Columbia University

Contributions to Education

Teachers College Series

No. 178

AMS PRESS

NEW YORK

A STUDY OF THE MILL SCHOOLS OF NORTH CAROLINA

BY

JOHN HARRISON COOK, Ph.D.

Teachers College, Columbia University
Contributions to Education, No. 178

Published by
Teachers College, Columbia University
New York City
1925

Library of Congress Cataloging in Publication Data

Cook, John Harrison, 1881-
   A study of the mill schools of North Carolina.

   Reprint of the 1925 ed., issued in series: Teachers
College, Columbia University. Contributions to
education, no. 178.
   Originally presented as the author's thesis,
Columbia.
   Includes bibliographical references.
   1. Labor and laboring classes--Education--North
Carolina. 2. Cotton manufacture--North Carolina.
I. Title. II. Series: Columbia University. Teachers
College. Contributions to education, no. 178.
LC5052.N8C6 1972   301.36   73-176668
ISBN 0-404-55178-5

301.36
C77s
85763
Nov. 1973

Reprinted by Special Arrangement with Teachers
College Press, New York, New York

From the edition of 1925, New York
First AMS edition published in 1972
Manufactured in the United States

AMS PRESS, INC.
NEW YORK, N. Y.   10003

ACKNOWLEDGMENTS

The author is under obligation to several people for assistance, criticisms and suggestions. He is grateful for the help, guidance and sympathetic interest of his dissertation committee consisting of Dr. Paul R. Mort, Dr. William H. Kilpatrick, Dr. Edward S. Reisner and Dr. F. G. Bonser. He is also indebted to Dr. N. L. Engelhardt for valuable suggestions; to Dr. J. A. Highsmith of the North Carolina College for Women for assistance in giving intelligence tests and for helpful advice; and to Professor J. Arthur Dunn of the same institution for his assistance in editing.

He is also under obligation to several county superintendents, supervisors and principals of mill schools in North Carolina for assistance and coöperation. He wishes to mention especially Miss Sue Reece, Supervisor of Rowan County, Miss Carrie Glenn, Supervisor of Gaston County, Superintendent W. J. Sloan, of Kannapolis, and Miss Eva J. Cox, his secretary.

Most of all, the author is indebted to his wife, Ethel Smith Cook, for continuous assistance at all stages of the work and for the encouragement which led to the undertaking and completion of this study.

J. H. C.

CONTENTS

TABLES

CHAPTER I

DEVELOPMENT OF THE COTTON MILL INDUSTRY IN NORTH CAROLINA AND FACTS CONCERNING MILL SCHOOLS

THE cotton manufacturing industry is developing very rapidly in the South and especially so in North Carolina. In value of product, capital invested and number of spindles, North Carolina leads the southern states and in a comparison with all the states of the Union is second only to Massachusetts. In rate and amount of growth, as judged by increase in the number of spindles, North Carolina has in the last decade surpassed Massachusetts and all of the other states. North Carolina leads them all in the number of cotton mills. There are now in the state 5,918,538 spindles and 386 cotton mills.[1] In addition there are 142 knitting and hosiery mills.[2]

As a result of the growth of the cotton manufacturing industry, a large number of new villages and towns have been developed and outlying sections of cities have been built up. The education of the children of the workers in the cotton mills has become one of the vital problems of education in the South. This increase in school population by the establishment of new mills is usually so sudden that planning has generally been with temporary rather than permanent objectives in view. As a result, adequate school programs have not been planned for children of mill workers. As the mill workers live in segregated "mill districts" or "mill towns," the kind of school that "mill children" attend is not often of direct concern to other members of the community. The mill workers are, in a large majority of cases, from rural districts where educational advantages were during their youth among the poorest in America. Lacking knowledge of educational standards and without cultural ideals, the mill worker is

[1] North Carolina Report, Department of Labor and Printing, 1923–24, No. 34, Chap. I.
[2] North Carolina Report, Department of Labor and Printing, 1921–22, No. 33, page 65, Chap. II.

1

content with an inferior type of school. It has come to be the expected and accepted thing that mill schools are not offering educational opportunities equal to those offered in towns of similar size or in more favored rural communities. It is the purpose of this study to find out the facts in the "mill school" situation of North Carolina and, if necessary, to seek for causes of the poor conditions and offer suggestions for improvement.

There are two methods of providing educational facilities for the children of mill workers living on the outskirts of cities and special chartered school districts. One is that of letting the children be absorbed into the established school systems. This plan gives the children of mill workers every public educational advantage enjoyed by other children of the city and counteracts the tendencies toward class cleavage. Unfortunately, this method is followed only in rare instances. The other and more usual practice, when a mill is built near a city or special-chartered district, is that of establishing a school for mill workers. Such schools are independent of the control of the city or special-chartered school systems.

But in every case, the mill school is inferior to the school already established. Except in the case of North Charlotte and Hoskins, these mill schools offer work for only a seven years' program. Under this plan the children in mill schools must pay some tuition, if they wish to enter the special-chartered or city schools in order to take work above the seventh grade.

When a new mill town is built, a school must be organized to provide for the children of mill workers. Sometimes the previously existing rural or small village schools are absorbed into the mill schools. In this way a few mill schools have children other than those of the mill workers enrolled.

For the purpose of this study, only school systems in which the children of mill workers constitute a majority of the school enrollment will be considered mill schools. This will eliminate from the scope of this study, individual school buildings to which the children of mill workers are assigned, if these are included in a school system less than fifty per cent of which is composed of mill children.

The growth of mill schools has kept pace with the increase in the number of mills. There are at present 119 mill schools in North Carolina. These schools are located principally in the Piedmont region of North Carolina. There are mill schools in thirty-six counties. Of these counties, twenty-nine are considered Piedmont counties; five are in the coastal plain; two are mountain counties.

Of these 119 independent mill schools, 38 either are located within the city limits or border upon a special-chartered school district, which maintains an accredited high school. There are three such schools maintained within the corporate limits of Greensboro, three each on the edge of Lexington, Lumberton, Marion, Shelby and Gastonia; two each bordering Concord, Charlotte, Rockingham, Hickory and Roxboro; and one each touching Hendersonville, Salisbury, Monroe, Chapel Hill, Burlington, Albemarle, Troy, Lincolnton and North Wilkesboro. The remaining mill schools are in towns built up as a result of the location of mills in them.

The first cotton mill was built near Graham in 1845. Until 1887, there were only fifteen cotton mills in North Carolina. These were small mills located chiefly in Alamance, Randolph and Richmond counties. The labor supply was, until then, drawn from the immediate neighborhood and no new social or educational problem was added. In 1887, the Cannon Manufacturing Company began building mills on a larger scale in Concord and Kannapolis. Others followed with larger cotton mills. A steady increase in the number of mills was maintained until 1896, when several large mills were built. The size and number of mills increased steadily from 1900 until 1908.[3] From 1914 on, the number of mills and those employed in the mills has increased very rapidly. In 1924, 48,609 men, 30,347 women, and 4,772 children between fourteen and sixteen years of age were employed in the cotton mills of North Carolina.

The growth of the cotton mill industry in North Carolina since 1885, together with the increasing tendency since then to concentrate mills in certain favored centers, has necessitated that employers go far from the immediate locality for the labor supply. The workers in the cotton mills are for the most part semi-skilled and unskilled laborers and are drawn chiefly from the ranks of farm hands and those with irregular employment living in small villages and rural districts. Workers in cotton mills of North Carolina come chiefly from the rural districts of the Piedmont and mountain counties of North Carolina and neighboring states.

[3] North Carolina Report, Department of Labor and Printing, 1923–24, No. 34, Chap. I.

TABLE I

MISCELLANEOUS DATA CONCERNING MILL SCHOOLS IN NORTH CAROLINA

Name of School	County	Date	Number of Grades	Enrollment	Length of Term in Days	Supported By	Buildings Owned By
1. Elmira............	Alamance	1896	9	247	160	Local Tax	County
2. Glencoe..........	"	1901	7	63	120	None	"
3. Glenwood........	"	....	7	59	120	"	"
4. Glen Raven......	"	1904	7	74	120	"	"
5. Haw River.......	"	1917	11	352	180	Local Tax	"
6. Altamahaw-Ossipee	"	....	11	271	180	" "	"
7. Saxapahaw.......	"	....	7	142	160	" "	"
8. Caroline-Hopedale	"	1878	7	79	160	" "	"
9. Swepsonville......	"	1895	7	146	160	" "	"
10. Bladenboro.......	Bladen	1913	11	416	180	" "	"
11. Woodfin..........	Buncombe	1888	11	......	180	Subsidy	Mills
12. Brown-Norcutt....	Cabarrus	1906	7	228	160	Local Tax	County
13. Hartsell..........	"	1907	7	332	150	Local Tax	County
14. Kannapolis.......	Cabarrus-Rowan	1888	11	1,502	180	Subsidy	"
15. Valmead.........	Caldwell	1908	7	192	120	Local Tax	"
16. Whitnel..........	"	1908	9	250	143	" "	"
17. Hudson..........	"	1905	10	238	160	" "	"
18. Rhodiss..........	"	1921	7	215	140	" "	"
19. Dudley Shoals....	"	1907	10	179	160	" "	"
20. Brookford........	Catawba	1918					
21. Longview.........	"	1917	.....	304	160	Local Tax	County
22. West Hickory.....	"	1904	11	480	160	" "	"
23. Kings Mountain...	Cleveland	1914	7	391	160	" "	"
24. Eastside Shelby...	"	1919	7	120	120	None	Mills
25. South Shelby.....	"	1912	7	103	160	Subsidy	"
26. Dover............	"	1923	7	101	120	None	
27. Hope Mills.......	Cumberland	1917	11	356	180	Local Tax	County
28. Dakotah.........	Davidson	1910	7	112	160	Subsidy	Mills
29. Erlanger.........	"	1915	7	261	180	"	"
30. Nokomis.........	"	1902	7	158	160	Local Tax	County
31. Cooleemee........	Davie	....	11	763	160	" "	"
32. West Durham....	Durham	1890	11	660	180	" "	"
33. Hanes...........	Forsyth	1915	7	281	180	Subsidy	Mills
34. Lowell...........	Gaston	1893	11	499	160	Local Tax	County
35. Dallas...........	"	....	11	403	160	" "	"
36. Ranlo...........	"	1918	11	500	160	" "	"
37. Cramerton.......	"	1908	9	524	160	" "	Mills
38. Belmont.........	"	1902	11	1,015	180	" "	County
39. North Belmont....	"	....	7	352	180	" "	"
40. Bessemer City....	"	1909	11	780	160	" "	"
41. Cherryville......	"	1897	11	793	160	" "	"
42. Victory..........	"	1920	6	336	160	" "	"
43. South Gastonia...	"	1921	7	335	160	" "	"
44. Stanley..........	"	1919	11	325	160	" "	"
45. High Shoals......	"	1921	9	180	160	" "	"
46. Mount Holly.....	"	1884	11	800	180	" "	"
47. Flint-Grove......	"	1916	9	339	160	" "	"
48. Bakers...........	"	....	7	55	160	" "	"
49. Harden..........	"	1888	7	97	120	None	"
50. Myrtle..........	"	1919	7	267	180	Local Tax	"
51. Spencer Mt......	"	1896	6	105	160	" "	"
52. Tuskaseege.......	"	1884	7	82	160	" "	"
53. McAdenville......	"	1883	7	228	160	" "	"
54. Proximity........	Guilford	1901	7	531	180	Subsidy	Mills
55. Revolution.......	"	1908	7	377	173	"	"
56. White Oak.......	"	1906	7	783	173	"	"
57. Gibsonville.......	"	1902	11	567	160	Local Tax	County
58. Roanoke Rapids..	Halifax	1897	11	1,342	180	" "	"
59. Duke............	Harnett	1893	11	526	180	" "	"
60. East Flat Rock...	Henderson	1909	11	293	180	" "	"
61. Tuxedo..........	"	1908	7	68	120	None	"
62. Balfour..........	"	....					
63. East Monbo......	Iredell	1921	7	54	120	None	County
64. Rhyne Memorial..	Lincoln	....	7	155	160	Local Tax	"
65. Laboratory.......	"	1889	7	161	140	" "	"
66. South Side.......	"	1897	7	81	120	None	"
67. Long Shoals......	"	1897	7	130	120	"	"
68. Near Marion.....	McDowell	1915	7				
69. Near Marion.....	"	1917	7				
70. Near Marion.....	"	1920	7				

Name of School	County	Date	Number of Grades	Enrollment	Length of Term in Days	Supported By	Buildings Owned By
71. North Charlotte...	Mecklenburg	1903	9	341	180	Local Tax	County
72. Hoskins.........	"	1909	9	412	160	" "	"
73. Cornelius........	"	1889	11	413	160	" "	"
74. Huntersville.....	"	1889	11	515	160	" "	"
75. Paw Creek......	"	1914	11	388	160	" "	"
76. Capelsie.........	Montgomery	1889	7	102	160	" "	"
77. Tuckertown......	"	1922	7	73	120	None	"
78. W. Rocky Mount..	Nash	1879	7	......	160	Subsidy	Mills
79. Carrboro........	Orange	....	7	234	166	Local Tax	County
80. East Roxboro.....	Person	1901	7	65	180	Subsidy	Mills
81. Longhurst........	"	1909	7	221	160	"	"
82. Lynn...........	Polk	....	7	113	160	Local Tax	County
83. Franklinville......	Randolph	1865	11	263	160	" "	"
84. Ramseur........	"	1851	11	380	160	" "	"
85. Randleman......	"	1912	11	433	160	" "	"
86. Central Falls.....	"	1913	7	114	120	None	"
87. Coleridge........	"	1905	7	171	120	"	"
88. Staley..........	"	1919	8	143	120	"	"
89. Cedar Falls......	"	....	7	109	120	"	"
90. Worthville.......	"	1914	7	125	120	"	"
91. Cordova........	Richmond	....	7	154	160	Local Tax	Mills
92. Rohanen........	"	....	7	641	160	" "	County
93. Pee Dee........	"	1875	7	283	160	" "	"
94. Lemorae........	"	1883	7	73	140	" "	"
95. Roberdell........	"	1883	7	150	160	" "	"
96. Ledbea..........	"	1888	7	63	140	" "	"
97. E. Lumberton.....	Robeson	1901	7	205	120	None	Mills
98. Jennings........	"	1907	7	73	120	"	"
99. Near Lumberton..	"	1907	7	......	......	"	"
100. Mayodan........	Rockingham	1896	7	540	160	Local Tax	County
101. Leaksville-Spray (5 schools)......	"	1898	11	2,807	180	" "	"
106. China Grove......	Rowan	1897	7	283	160	" "	"
107. Landis...........	"	1901	11	290	160	" "	"
108. Rowan Mills......	"	1921	7	78	160	Subsidy	Mills
109. Yadkin..........	"	1921	7	46	180	"	"
110. Caroleen........	Rutherford	1888	7	338	160	Local Tax	County
111. Henrietta........	"	1892	11	462	160	" "	"
112. Alexander.......	"	1918	7	202	160	" "	"
113. Spindale........	"	1918	11	460	160	" "	"
114. Cliffside........	"	1905	11	804	160	" "	Mills
115. Avondale........	"	1897	8	173	180	" "	County
116. Wicassett-Efird....	Stanley	1897	7	1,146	160	Subsidy	Mills
117. Icemorlee........	Union	1907	7	110	180	"	"
118. Falls of Neuse.....	Wake	1913	7	98			
119. Near Wilkesboro...	Wilkes	1920	7	......	160	Local Tax	County

Mill villages have been built for the workers brought into the mills. Schools of some sort had to be provided for the children of the mill villages. To induce capitalists to locate mills near cities, concessions, in the way of exemptions from local city and school taxes, were often granted. It was usually much cheaper for mills to provide inferior schools for the children of their workers rather than to pay school taxes. Because of conditions arising from the use of such methods, mill schools became a problem about 1890 which has increased in scope and importance since.

There are now enrolled in the mill schools of North Carolina 36,222 pupils. The location of these schools is indicated on the accompanying map. The enrollment, the number of grades taught,

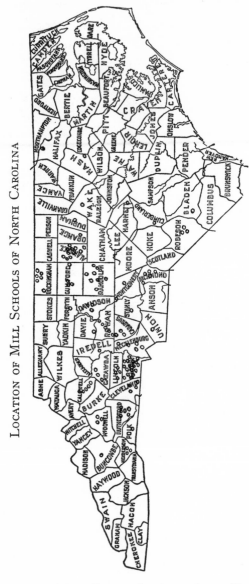

LOCATION OF MILL SCHOOLS OF NORTH CAROLINA

the location, date of founding or the time when mill children first constituted a majority of the school, the method of support and the ownership of the school building in the case of each mill school of North Carolina will be found in Table I on pages 4 and 5.

CHAPTER II

CONTROL, LENGTH OF TERM AND COMPARATIVE COST OF MILL SCHOOLS

THERE are three classes of school districts in North Carolina: local non-taxing school districts, local tax-paying school districts and special-chartered school districts. There is no difference in the organization of the taxing and non-taxing school districts, except that in the taxing school districts the county support of schools is supplemented by a local tax, while in non-taxing school districts the county funds are the sole source of public support for schools. In special-chartered schools, the control of the schools is independent of the county board of education and is directly or indirectly in the hands of the people of the school district.

In local non-taxing and taxing school districts, the committee-men are appointed by the county board of education.[4] Committee-men have the power to choose teachers for the schools of their respective districts, subject to the approval of the county super-intendent.[5] The expenditure of funds raised by local tax is controlled by the local committeemen of taxing districts. Requisitions for maintenance and supplies are made by local committee-men to the county board but must be approved by the county superintendent. County boards of education through county superintendents have warrant both by law and custom to exercise considerable control over schools included within the county system. Yet by appointing committeemen whose first allegiance is not to the schools of the district, the power of the county super-intendent to help such schools may be diminished or completely nullified.

Mill schools in respect to degree of control exercised over them by mill owners or officials may be divided into three types.

1. The special-chartered schools of North Carolina are more

[4] The Public School Law of North Carolina, Codification of 1923, Art. 10, Sec. 123; Art. 11, Sec. 144.
[5] The Public School Law of North Carolina, Codification of 1923, Art. 10, Sec. 130.

responsive to the direct control of the people of the community served than is any other type of school.[6] There are in North Carolina 125 such school systems varying in enrollment from 217 to 11,996. As a class these schools are the most efficient of the state. The influence of mill owners and officials over the policies of special-chartered mill schools is reduced to a minimum. There are seven mill schools among the 119 in this class. They are: Roanoke Rapids, Bessemer City, Cherryville, Franklinville, Ramseur, Haw River and West Hickory. In each of these schools the mill schools absorbed rural or village schools into the school system. Largely through the influence of citizens not connected with the management of the mills, the organization of the schools has been more democratic than in mill schools that lack the support of many citizens who are not connected with the mills. In each special chartered mill school, there are eleven grades, including a state accredited high school.

2. The second type of mill school classified with respect to the degree of control exercised by the mill owners, is made up of local school districts in which mill owners or officials have only such control as may be had by other committeemen. In every local school district from which reports were received, the majority of the committeemen were mill owners or their representatives. The control of mill owners over such schools is secured and held by the appointment of owners or officials as committeemen. Often those who do not live within the school district are appointed to serve in this capacity. The degree of control which mill owners exercise over the policies and the length of the course in such schools varies considerably in different schools and different counties.

3. The type of mill schools over which the mill owners exercise most control is that in which the schools are subsidized in lieu of local taxes, or in which the school building is owned by the mill companies, or in which both of these conditions obtain. There are 26 mill schools of the 109 from which there are accurate reports in which one or the other of these conditions prevail. In fifteen of these instances the mill owners own the school buildings and subsidize the school instead of paying a local tax to supplement county funds. In the majority of these cases, the mill officials assume the powers of committeemen with the informal consent of

[6] Records of North Carolina Department of Public Instruction.

the county board. In at least four instances, a mill official is termed superintendent of school and appoints teachers and directs policies of the school with the consent of the county superintendent. In four instances the county pays rent to the mill owners for the use of the buildings and in at least five cases, the teachers are given their pay checks by mill officials just as in the case of the payment of other mill employees. In three instances, at least, the funds raised by the county for the support of schools in the respective districts are paid to the mill companies at the end of the school year. In every instance where the mills own the building and subsidize the schools in lieu of local tax, there are only seven grades in the school system.

The control of mill schools is merely a part of the general program of control which mill owners have with respect to those who live in the village. Villages are not incorporated except in rare instances. One mill community has a population of over 8,000 and is not incorporated. Order is maintained in unincorporated communities of large population by deputy sheriffs subsidized by mill companies. County government takes over the other functions usually exercised by municipalities. There is no necessity for mill workers to think of problems of local government, as every public utility is controlled by the mills.

In the typical mill community, all real estate is owned by the mill companies. It is impossible for mill workmen to buy homes. Without a contract for a definite tenure, they live in houses owned by the mills. The butcher, grocer, merchant, physician, dentist, preacher, teacher and welfare worker must live in houses owned by the mill company. Leases for offices and stores are for no longer than one year. Often churches must be built on real estate owned by the company. Regulations as to what may be grown in the garden and as to how often the lawn must be trimmed are often in effect. There is no place for meetings to discuss topics under ban. The expression of one who installed this system into several mill villages was "The school is a part of our business."

The degree of control which the mill owners have over the mill workers is greater than that which usually exists in other industries. To the unlimited power of summarily and arbitrarily dismissing employees is joined that of ejecting them from their homes, which are mill owned. Should an employee be bold enough in the face of such difficulties to suggest the discussion of common complaints or problems, there would be no building in which a meeting could be held. Should there be a referendum on a local school tax, or a liberal candidate for legislature, the open ballot in use in the state permits the owner to know how each employee votes. This same voting system reinforces the influence of mill owners with both those who make and those who execute the laws. In a typical mill village, the mill worker is without the semblance of influence in municipal affairs. His period of residence in the village is uncertain and his interests can be only those of a transient. Every privilege and improvement must come from mill owners. Considerable power over school policies and the teaching force helps to complete and continue such a scheme of control by mill owners.

By letters from or personal conferences with eighty-one principals of mill schools of all classes, an effort was made to determine whether or not the mill owners sought to influence teachers to.discourage children from remaining in high schools or attending high school. Not an instance of this was found. In twelve instances the attitude of mill officials was that of encouragement toward high school attendance. In three instances, mill owners or mill officials were in pronounced opposition. In the other sixty-six instances the matter was one about which the mill owners were reported to have no declared policy one way or the other. A mill official who is also school superintendent of the school department of the mill states that the only instruction mill owners insist upon is that the teachers must uphold work in the mill as an honorable vocation.

The constitution of North Carolina requires every school district of the state to maintain school for a term of six months.[7] Free tuition for this period each year is guaranteed every child between six and twenty-one years of age.[8] The county tax for schools provides the funds for this term. A term beyond this period of time must be paid for by funds raised by the school district. Of 112 mill schools which reported on the length of term, 19 have a term of 6 months; 6 a term of 7 months; 59 a term of 8 months; 3 a term of 173 days; and 25 a term of nine months.

[7] Constitution of North Carolina, Art. 11, Sec. 29.
[8] The Public School Law of North Carolina, Codification of 1923, Part I, Art. L, Sec. I.

For the school year of 1924, there were 54.4 of the white children of North Carolina who had a school term of eight months or more.[9] The sentiment for a term of eight months in North Carolina is such that industries which need employees of any skill must provide an eight months' term of school. Yet in twenty-five mill schools, the length of term is less than eight months.

A comparison of what mill companies gain by paying subsidy or local tax rather than the school tax of the city of which they are virtually a part, has been made. Data were secured with reference to sixteen mill schools in villages actually or virtually a part of cities which they bordered. If the city tax were paid, the children would have the educational advantages granted to the children of cities, including that of high school education without tuition. The data were secured from the county records of Guilford, Orange, Alamance, Forsyth, Davidson, Stanley, Rowan, Cabarrus, Mecklenburg and Union counties, and include all schools of the type mentioned located in the counties named. These counties are contiguous and form a broad belt of territory from Virginia to the South Carolina line through the heart of the mill region of North Carolina.

Table II shows how much the school funds of the various cities lose and how much the mill companies gain when subsidies are used to provide for a term beyond six months.

TABLE II

Costs of Subsidized Mill Schools Compared With What It Would Be If Included in Contiguous City Schools

Schools	City Tax Rate for Schools in Addition to School Tax of County—Cents per $100.00	Valuation of Mill Property	Amount Which Would be Raised by City School Tax	Amount Paid for Additional Term	Gain to Mills
A......	37	$4,500,000	$16,650	$3,120	$13,530
B and C	37	8,983,820	33,240	6,422	26,818
D......	29	2,324,445	6,740	2,200	4,541
E......	54	775,512	4,188	640	3,547
F......	55	300,000	1,650	200	1,450
G......	60	590,706	3,544	500	3,044
H......	38	1,230,860	4,677	901	3,776
I.......	40	2,108,684	8,034	2,400	6,034
X......	30	4,759,852	13,270	6,406	6,864

[9] Biennial Report of Superintendent of Public Instruction of North Carolina, 1922–24, p. 19.

Table III shows how much mill companies gain by having a local tax levied to provide funds for the term beyond six months rather than paying the city tax.

TABLE III

Costs of Local Tax Mill Schools Compared With What It Would Be If Included in Contiguous City Schools

School	City School Tax Rate	Local District School Tax Rate	Valuation of Mill Property	Amount of Support Beyond County Tax	Gain to Mills
J........	37¾	30	$214,772	$644	$166
K........	30	25	2,036,650	5,092	1,018
L........	30	25	1,302,235	3,456	651
M.......	75	60	789,099	4,734	1,183
N........	38	15	460,760	691	975
O........	54	15	450,800	676	1,758

The amount which the mills mentioned in Table II raise by subsidy to provide for extra term is 24.6 per cent of what would be raised for school purposes if these mills were included in the special-chartered school districts which they border. In cases where a local tax is levied to provide for the extra term, the mills pay 73 per cent of what they would pay were they included in the special chartered districts. With the addition of the local tax the number of grades provided for is likely to be more; one-half of the mill schools in Table II have nine grades. Those in Table I each provide only for work through the seven grades. It appears that if the mill schools are segregated from the city schools, better educational advantages are more likely to be secured by local tax rather than by subsidy. The system of subsidies and segregation prevents all property of the community from contributing to the education of all the community. The mill children are also denied opportunity for a free high school education such as is given to other children in the city.

In twenty-four instances out of one hundred and nine cases reported, the mills own the school buildings of the mill schools. This policy is bad for two reasons. One is that the mill owners are in a better position to dictate policies to school authorities. The other is that the mill owners, after providing for their own immediate village, are not so ready to have the property of the mills contribute to the building of schoolhouses in other sections of the country. County-wide plans for building are recommended very strongly by the Department of Public Instruction of the State of North Carolina. As there is not a secret ballot in North Carolina, the influence of mill owners to defeat such plans could be considerable. It would be more just for the mill schools to share in the funds raised by all the property of the county.

In the type of schools over which mill owners have the least influence, every mill school has an eleven-grade system. In the type of school over which mill owners have the most influence, every school has a seven-grade system. This indicates the direction of control by mill owners over the policies of school systems. As there is a conflict between the economic interests of mill owners and the educational interests of mill children, it is unwise to add to the potential control of mill owners over the policies of mill schools. Local committeemen for mill schools should not be chosen from those whose financial interests clash with the adequate support of the school; nor should they be selected from those whose economic interests are furthered by having children leave school at an early age. The greater the degree of control by mill owners, the less likely are the schools to have a course of study beyond the seventh grade or any other advantages beyond the minimum legal requirements.

The purpose of mill owners in exercising an unusually large degree of control over mill schools as gathered from reports from principals and as understood from results of this study may be classified under four heads:

1. To control schools merely as a part of the general scheme of control over all phases of community life,
2. To facilitate and strengthen the control referred to in (1),
3. To keep the costs of schools low, and
4. Prevent schools from drawing too many potential laborers from the mill.

Two evident results of mill control over schools are low cost and short courses of study.

CHAPTER III

GENERAL INTELLIGENCE AND ACHIEVEMENTS OF THE CHILDREN OF MILL SCHOOLS

Two groups were chosen for testing the general intelligence and achievements of the children of the mill schools; one on the basis of age, the other on that of grade. In order that there might be the least possible amount of selection entering into the choice of those in the age group, the children of eleven years of age were chosen. As a large number of the mill schools have only seven grades, to have chosen an older group would have left out some of the brighter pupils who might possibly be in the eighth grade elsewhere. A younger group would be less likely to reveal native ability and achievements in standard tests. Had not the process of selection entered in, the twelve-year-old group would have perhaps yielded better results. But it was necessary to get children from all sorts of mill schools.

In choosing the schools [10] in which tests were to be given, it was decided to consider two factors: One that the schools chosen be thoroughly representative mill schools; and the other that the schools be distributed with reference to geography. The latter factor is important in North Carolina, as the state is divided into three geographical regions because of the topography of the state. The people in each region differ widely in politics, educational advantages and economic ideals. It was decided to give tests in the five that seemed to have the largest number of children in mill schools and then choose other counties, if need be, on the basis of geography. The counties chosen were Gaston, Alamance, Guilford, Cabarrus and Rutherford. The schools to be chosen in the county were decided upon because of information from the county superintendents as to what schools were most nearly exclusively made up of mill children. Two schools were tested in Gaston County on account of the large number of mill schools and the large enrollment of mill children in the county.[11] After

---

[10] The name of the schools can be secured upon request from the writer or Teachers College, Columbia University.   [11] See list of mill schools.

schools were tested in these counties, it was discovered that the eastern part of the state was not represented in quite the same proportion as the western. Carrboro, just within the eastern edge of the main mill belt, was added to the list of schools tested.[12]

The schools tested were as follows: Proximity, a seven-grade system within the corporate limits, but without the school district of Greensboro; Kannapolis, an eleven-grade system with school buildings in both Cabarrus and Rowan counties, and in the largest mill town in the state; Ranlo, an eleven-grade system in Gaston County, about five miles from Gastonia; the seventh grade of Cramerton in Gaston County, a nine-grade system; and the eleven-year-olds of Belmont, an eleven-grade system in Gaston County;[13] Caroleen, part of a coördinate eleven-grade system in Rutherford County, at the foot of the Blue Ridge; Elmira, a nine-grade system virtually included in the city of Burlington, Alamance County; and Carrboro, a seven-grade system just without the chartered school district, Chapel Hill, Orange County.

The test used to determine the general intelligence was Scale B, Form I, National Intelligence Tests. The tests were given by Dr. J. A. Highsmith, professor of psychology, North Carolina College for Women, and by the writer.

The number of eleven-year-old children from the different schools distributed as to grade are given in Table IV.

TABLE IV

GRADE DISTRIBUTION OF ELEVEN-YEAR-OLD PUPILS TESTED AND THE NUMBER FROM EACH SCHOOL SYSTEM

School System	Grade I	Grade II	Grade III	Grade IV	Grade V	Grade VI	Grade VII	Grade VIII	Total
Kannapolis	.....	2	27	47	32	25	2	.....	135
Proximity	.....	3	7	24	18	7	.....	.....	59
Belmont	1	10	19	15	19	12	4	.....	80
Caroleen	2	2	5	4	6	3	1	.....	23
Carrboro	.....	.....	6	6	13	2	.....	.....	27
Elmira	.....	2	3	10	11	2	.....	.....	28
Ranlo	2	11	19	11	13	.....	.....	1	57
Total	5	30	86	117	112	51	7	1	409

[12] See map of the state of North Carolina for the location of the centers tested.

[13] The seventh grade of Belmont was not tested because a truck brought in several pupils from the outside to this grade. The tests given to some eleven-year-olds in Cramerton were rejected because some of the lower grades had double sessions and all the eleven-year-olds were not included.

The eleven-year-old pupils of each system tested were all included in the group brought together for the testing. When a child through utter inability to read or write could do nothing with the test, his paper was not included in the results. If any question was answered, the paper was included in tabulating the results. All seventh-grade children in these systems, with the exceptions mentioned, were tested.

In the age-grade tables compiled [14] from the different mill schools from which this information was secured, there were in all 1837 eleven-year-old pupils. A comparison is made in Table V of the distribution in the different grades of those tested with that of the total number of eleven-year-old pupils included in the age-grade tables.

TABLE V

COMPARISON OF DISTRIBUTION OF ELEVEN-YEAR-OLD PUPILS TESTED WITH THAT REPRESENTED BY THE TOTAL OF ELEVEN-YEAR-OLDS SECURED IN THE AGE-GRADE TABLES

	Grade I	Grade II	Grade III	Grade IV	Grade V	Grade VI	Grade VII	Grade VIII
Age-Grade Table Distribution ...	68	158	360	516	463	221	41	10
Percentage of Above Total in Each Grade....	3.7	8.7	19.6	27.6	25.4	12.1	2.3	.6
Percentage of Those Tested in Each Grade..	1.3	7.4	21.0	28.5	27.3	12.5	1.7	.3

This shows how nearly the group tested was representative of the entire eleven-year-old group as distributed by grades in the mill schools. The group tested was even more nearly representative than would appear from the above table when the fact is considered that ten papers were not included in the tests because no questions were answered. These children were probably in the first or second grade.

The summary of scores by schools is shown in Tables VI and VII; the summary of the results by grades is given in Table VIII.

The intelligence quotients were calculated in accordance with the directions given in the manual of directions last issued by

[14] See Tables XXI to XXIII.

TABLES VI AND VII

Summary of the Scores Made in the Different Schools Tested on the National Intelligence Tests, Scale B, Form I

Table VI
Eleven-Year-Old Pupils

Number of School	Average Score
1	61
2	57
3	48
4	54½
5	50
7	65

Average Score of Pupils Tested 56

Normal Score for Eleven-Year-Old Children 96

Number of Pupils Tested.... 409

Table VII
Seventh-Grade Pupils

Number of School	Average Score
1	106
2	97.4
3	106
5	101
6	97
8	112.5

Average Score of Pupils Tested 100.9

Standard Score for Seventh Grade 120

Number of Pupils Tested.... 162

TABLE VIII

Scores Made on National Intelligence Tests, Scale B, Form I, by Children in Certain Mill Schools in North Carolina Distributed by Grades

Scores	By Eleven-Year-Old Pupils									By Seventh-Grade Pupils
	Grade I	Grade II	Grade III	Grade IV	Grade V	Grade VI	Grade VII	Grade VIII	Total	
0– 9	5	9	5	1	.....	.....	.....	.....	20	
10– 19	.....	10	18	.....	.....	.....	.....	.....	28	
20– 29	.....	10	25	3	.....	.....	.....	.....	38	
30– 39	.....	1	22	12	1	.....	.....	.....	36	
40– 49	.....	.....	8	27	6	.....	.....	.....	41	
50– 59	.....	.....	6	31	17	2	.....	.....	56	1
60– 69	.....	.....	1	27	27	5	.....	.....	60	3
70– 79	.....	.....	.....	14	33	8	.....	.....	55	9
80– 89	.....	.....	1	0	19	10	2	.....	32	24
90– 99	.....	.....	.....	1	8	11	.....	.....	20	36
100–109	.....	.....	.....	1	1	7	1	.....	10	37
110–119	.....	.....	.....	.....	.....	6	.....	.....	6	29
120–129	.....	.....	.....	.....	.....	1	.....	.....	1	15
130–139	.....	.....	.....	.....	.....	1	4	.....	5	7
140–149	.....	.....	.....	.....	.....	.....	.....	.....	0	1
150–159	.....	.....	.....	.....	.....	.....	.....	1	1	
Total	5	30	86	117	112	51	7	1	409	162
Median	5	16	28	55	71.5	90.5	131.2	151	57.4	102.2
Standard for Grades	.....	.....	.....	77	96	110	120	138	.....	120
Standard for Eleven-Year-Old Pupils	.....	.....	.....	.....	.....	.....	.....	.....	96	

the director of the National Intelligence Tests.[15]   As the data
are insufficient to calculate accurately the intelligence quotients
of eleven-year-old children when the I.Q. is under 70, all results
lower than this are indicated by 70 —.

TABLE IX

INTELLIGENCE QUOTIENTS OF PUPILS OF CERTAIN MILL SCHOOLS IN NORTH
CAROLINA BASED ON THE NATIONAL INTELLIGENCE TESTS, SCALE B, FORM I

I. Q's	All Eleven-Year-Old Pupils	Eleven-Year-Old Pupils in the Fourth Grade or Above	Seventh-Grade Pupils
Under 70[16]	125	22	16
70–74	48	37	12
75–79	58	51	17
80–84	62	62	24
85–89	27	27	30
90–94	35	35	18
95–99	22	22	19
100–104	16	16	8
105–109	5	5	8
110–114	4	4	6
115–119	1	1	2
120–124	0	0	1
125–129	1	1	1
130–134	2	2	..
135–139	3	3	..
Total	409	288	162
Median	77.2	82.3	86.5

The scores made on the intelligence test were translated into
percentiles.   The percentile rank represents the position the pupils
would hold in a theoretical group of one hundred pupils.   The
poorest pupil is represented by 0.   The highest ranking in Table X
is 99.   This means that theoretically he is surpassed by only
one pupil in a hundred of a group taken at random.   In a normal
group, there should be about the same number of pupils in each
quartile.[17]

The average score of the 409 eleven-year-old pupils is 56; the

[15] Guy M. Whipple, *National Intelligence Tests Manual of Directions,* Supplement
No. 3, April, 1924, pp. 3-4 and Table 3.
[16] The distribution of the I.Q.'s of seventh-grade pupils under 70 follows: 62—2; 65—2;
66—3; 67—1; 68—6; and 69—2.
[17] Guy M. Whipple, *National Intelligence Tests Manual of Directions,* Supplement
No. 3, April, 1924, pp. 6-12.

TABLE X

PERCENTAGE RANKINGS OF PUPILS OF CERTAIN MILL SCHOOLS OF NORTH CAROLINA BASED ON THE NATIONAL INTELLIGENCE TESTS, SCALE B, FORM I *

Per-centile Rank	I	II	III	Per-centile Rank	I	II	III	Per-centile Rank	I	II	III	Per-centile Rank	I	II	III
0	26	1	....	26	7	7	3	51	....	....	....	76	2	2	...
1	26	1	....	27	4	4	2	52	2	2	1	77	....	....	...
2	22	4	1	28	10	10	1	53	....	....	2	78	....	....	2
3	18	3	....	29	4	4	2	54	1	1	....	79	1	1	...
4	13	1	5	30	4	4	1	55	1	1	1	80	....	....	...
5	19	12	7	31	4	4	2	56	2	2	....	81	....	....	...
6	16	11	3	32	6	6	2	57	....	....	....	82	....	....	...
7	9	8	6	33	3	3	1	58	1	1	2	83	....	....	1
8	23	18	8	34	3	3	1	59	....	....	....	84	....	....	...
9	17	16	3	35	2	2	1	60	3	2	1	85	....	....	...
10	14	13	4	36	....	....	3	61	3	3	....	86	....	....	...
11	12	10	6	37	2	2	4	62	....	....	1	87	1	1	...
12	11	8	4	38	5	5	3	63	....	....	1	88	....	....	...
13	5	5	3	39	1	1	....	64	....	....	2	89	....	....	...
14	11	11	8	40	2	2	1	65	1	1	1	90	2	2	...
15	4	4	5	41	2	2	1	66	....	....	....	91	1	1	1
16	4	4	3	42	....	....	....	67	1	1	1	92	....	....	...
17	20	20	3	43	2	2	3	68	1	1	....	93	1	1	...
18	4	4	....	44	3	3	2	69	....	....	1	94	1	1	...
19	10	10	5	45	4	4	1	70	....	....	1	95	....	....	...
20	4	4	4	46	1	1	....	71	2	2	2	96	....	....	...
21	12	12	6	47	....	....	3	72	....	....	....	97	....	....	...
22	4	4	3	48	2	2	3	73	....	....	2	98	....	....	...
23	2	2	2	49	3	3	....	74	1	1	1	99	1	1	...
24	1	1	3	50	1	1	3	75	....	....	....	100	....	....	...
25	1	1	3												
Total	308	188	95	Total	72	72	43	Total	19	18	20	Total	10	10	4
Percent in Each Quartile	75.3	65.3	58.6	......	17.6	25.0	26.5	......	4.7	6.3	12.4	......	2.4	3.4	2.5

*Number of Eleven-Year-Olds Tested, 409; Number of these in the Fourth Grade and above, 288; Number of Seventh Grade Pupils, 162.

I. Distribution of All Eleven-Year-Old Pupils.[18]
II. Distribution of All Eleven-Year-Old Pupils in the 4th Grade and Above.
III. Distribution of Seventh-Grade Pupils.

median score, 57.4. The standard score for a child eleven years and five months old is 96.[19]

Based on the same scores and standard, the median intelligence quotient of the eleven-year-old pupils is 77.2; that of the seventh-grade pupil is 82.3.

There should be about twenty-five per cent in each of the quartiles where the children are assigned percentile ranks as in Table X. But the results show a decided and unusual bunching in the lower quartiles; very few in the upper quartiles. There were of the eleven-year-old pupils 75.3 per cent in the lower

[18] In Table X, I signifies eleven-year-old pupils; II signifies those eleven-year-old pupils in the fourth grade or above; III seventh-grade pupils.
[19] *Ibid.*, p. 5.

quartile and 2.4 per cent in the upper. Of the seventh-grade pupils, 58.6 per cent were in the lower quartile and 25 per cent in the upper. A little more than three-fourths of the eleven-year-old pupils was in the lower quartile, as was considerably more than one-half of the seventh-grade pupils. In not a school tested was the average score near standard.

The evident conclusion is that in general intelligence the children attending mill schools rank very low. However, there must be other factors considered before these children can be judged commensurately low in native ability.

1. The standard score for eleven-year-old children was derived by giving the tests in the different grades and recording separately the scores of the eleven-year-old children. Usually, a National Intelligence Test is not given below the fourth grade. The group from which the norm was derived was, therefore, a selected group insofar as groups tested did not represent in due proportion the eleven-year-old children in the primary grades, who usually being retarded because of having less ability, would have lowered somewhat the norm. In the case of the group tested in the mill schools, there was no selection. When a test was given in the different mill schools, every child of eleven years of age took the test or at least attempted it. In Table VIII, it will be seen how the median score increased with the different grades from that of 5 for the eleven-year-old children of the first grade and 16 for those of the second to 90.5 and 131.2 for those of the same age in the sixth and seventh grades, respectively. The group of eleven-year-old children represents fairly proportionate distribution of children of that age among the different grades in the mill schools. The selection which was to some extent present in the group from which the standard was derived was absent in determining the results of this test.

2. The children tested in order to derive norms are usually children of city schools who are more or less accustomed to taking tests in which the time element is a large factor. They, therefore, have developed specific skill and aptitudes in taking time tests. After such experiences, a somewhat higher score will be made as a result of this specific training which may be carried over to new tests insofar as certain elements are identical. Children with the same general ability lacking this specific training will make a lower score. While the amount of this difference is not

definitely known, this element should be taken into account in interpreting the results given to the children in mill schools. In five of the schools tested, the children had never taken a standard test.

3. The home environment of these children has been unfavorable to acquiring useful information. The scarcity of reading material in the homes of the mill villages is responsible for lack of knowledge about many things going to make up general intelligence. The parents of the children unfortunately grew up where school facilities were either non-existent or very poor. Both parents of 240 children out of 246 came from the rural districts of states which at the time of the youth of the parents had educational facilities as poor as in any region of the United States.[20] The children living in segregated mill villages, in homes lacking educational stimulation, and in environments where all initiative is suppressed will be expected to be somewhat deficient in the informational element when examined by general intelligence tests.

In order that some results might be obtained unquestionably comparable to the standard score, a separate tabulation of scores made in the National Intelligence Tests was recorded for each grade. The medians for the different grades can be found by consulting Table VIII. Calculations are based separately on the group made up of children who were in the fourth grade or above. There were 288 of these children. These should have reading ability sufficient to enable them to make a score comparable to that of the standard.

The median score of the eleven-year-old children, who were in the fourth grade or above, was 67.5. The median intelligence quotient of this group was 82.3. The percentile ranking showed the distribution of this group to be 65.3 per cent of the number in the lowest quartile; 25 per cent in the next lowest quartile; 6.3 per cent in the second highest; and 3.4 per cent in the highest quartile. After selecting a group on the basis of this advancement in grades, the showing of even this group of eleven-year-old pupils was far below standard, whether estimated by absolute scores, intelligence quotients, or percentile ranking.

The seventh-grade children were also given the same general

[20] The parents of 221 of the children tested were reared in the rural districts of North Carolina, 10 in those of South Carolina, 4 in those of Virginia and 3 in those of Georgia.

intelligence test. The median score of the 162 seventh-grade pupils from the mill schools in which the tests were given was 102.2. The average score was 100.9. The normal score for this grade is 120. The average and median score of the pupils of every school tested was below standard from 7.5 to 23.0 points. The median intelligence quotient of the seventh-grade children was 86.5. The distribution of pupils by percentile ranking among the different quartiles beginning with the lowest 58.6 per cent, 26.5 per cent, 12.4 per cent and 2.5 per cent. The seventh-grade pupils also ranked below the standard in general intelligence according to each of the three methods to be used in comparisons. There is no selection to be reckoned with in comparing the results of the tests given the seventh-grade pupils with that of the standard.

According to comparisons made on the basis of age and grade, the children of mill schools fall far below the standard in general intelligence. This may be attributed to a repressive environment in community life, insufficient reading material in the homes and the school, and the native ability of this group, being below that of the average. However, there are marked exceptions to this general finding. The scores made by the eleven-year-old pupils in the sixth grade may, by allowing for exceptional elements already referred to, be considered as average. The eleven-year-old children in the seventh and eighth grades not only surpassed the standard score for their age, but went far beyond the standard of the seventh and eighth grades respectively. But the percentage of those who made scores up to standard or better is so small as not to affect the conclusion reached above.

To summarize, children of mill workers, considered as a social group more or less segregated from the remainder of the population by living in mill towns and attending mills. schools, fall considerably below standard in general intelligence. The native ability of this group, while lower than normal, is not as low as the scores would indicate.

Tests in arithmetical fundamentals and reading comprehension were also given to the eleven-year-old group and the pupils of the seventh grade. The test used in arithmetic was the Woody-McCall Mixed Fundamentals, Form I. That used in reading was the Thorndike-McCall Reading Scale, Form I. The group tested

TABLE XI

SCORES MADE BY ELEVEN-YEAR-OLD PUPILS OF CERTAIN MILL SCHOOLS
ON THE WOODY-MCCALL MIXED FUNDAMENTALS, FORM I,
DISTRIBUTED BY GRADES

Score	Grade I	Grade II	Grade III	Grade IV	Grade V	Grade VI	Grade VII	Grade VIII	Total
0	1								1
1	3	3	2						8
2	1	4	11	1					17
3		12	10	3					25
4		7	12	5					24
5			8	3					11
6			11	3	1				15
7		3	9	2					14
8		1	7	6					14
9			5	8	6	1			20
10			5	6	2				13
11			2	8	1	2			13
12			2	11	3	1			17
13			1	12	5	2			20
14			1	13	8				22
15				14	11	2	1		28
16				6	13	3			22
17			1	6	10	3			20
18			1	1	11	3			16
19				5	19	2	1		27
20				1	8	6			15
21				1	4	4	1		10
22				1	3	6			10
23			1		4	5	1	1	12
24					2	2			4
25						2	1		3
26						1			1
27						2			2
28						1			1
29									0
30							2		2
31						1			1
Total	5	30	89	116	111	49	7	1	408
Median	1	3.7	5.1	13.2	17.6	21	23	23	13.6
Standard for Grades			6.8	13.1	17.8	22.5	25.9	27.8	

Standard Score for Eleven-Year-Old Pupils...................... 22.6

in arithmetic and reading are, with the omission of four pupils, identical with those to whom the intelligence tests were given.

In order that the score made by the eleven-year-old pupils might be compared with the norm of the grade as well as that of age, the scores are recorded by grade in Table XI.

The scores made by pupils of the seventh grade on the test in arithmetic are distributed by schools and pupils in Table XII.

The distribution of ages of the seventh-grade children of the mill schools tested is as shown in Table XIII.

TABLE XII

Scores Made by the Pupils of the Seventh Grade in Certain Mill Schools on the Woody-McCall Mixed Fundamentals, Form I

Scores	School No. 1	School No. 2	School No. 3	School No. 5	School No. 6	School No. 8	Total
10.....							
11.....							...
12.....		2					2
13.....		1					1
14.....		1					1
15.....		1					1
16.....				1			1
17.....		2					2
18.....						1	1
19.....	1	3	3	1		2	10
20.....	1	7	1	1	2	1	13
21.....		8		1	1	2	12
22.....	1	8	2	5	2	2	20
23.....	2	3	2		1	2	10
24.....	1	6	1	1	1	1	11
25.....	2	11	2	6	1	2	24
26.....	2	9	4		1	2	19
27.....	2	5	2	2	1	1	13
28.....	2	2	1			1	6
29.....		3			1	1	5
30.....		3				1	4
31.....		1	1		1		3
32.....	1						1
33.....							0
34.....							0
Total....	15	76	19	18	12	20	160
Median..	25.2	24.3	25.2	23	23.5	23.5	24.5

Standard for Seventh Grade.................................... 25 9

TABLE XIII

AGES OF SEVENTH-GRADE MILL CHILDREN TAKING TESTS

Number of Pupils	Age
5	11
37	12
48	13
40	14
23	15
6	16
2	17
1	18
162	

Median Age ....13 years, 10 mo.

The median achievement of the seventh-grade pupils of mill schools in Woody-McCall Mixed Fundamentals is very close to the standard median for the seventh grade. The median of the mill children is 24.5 and the standard median is 25.9. Considering the fact that the tests were given as early as during the last week of October, the seventh-grade children of mill schools may be considered as practically up to standard in arithmetic fundamentals.

The median score made by eleven-year-old mill pupils in the Woody-McCall Mixed Fundamentals is 13.6. The standard median score for pupils of this age is 22.6. The eleven-year-old pupils in the third grade lack only 1.7 of being up to the median achievement of the third grade; those in the fourth grade are .1 ahead of the median standard for that grade; those in the fifth grade are .2 below their grade standard; those in the sixth, 1.5 below; and those in the seventh, 2.9 below. Using an estimate based upon grade norms, we find that the eleven-year-old children are very little, if any, below the standard in arithmetical fundamentals when one considers that the tests were given the last week in October. If the age norm is considered, these children are found to be 9 points below the standard.

The distribution of the scores of eleven-year-old pupils on the Thorndike-McCall Reading Scale, Form I, is given by grades in Table XIV. The median scores of the pupils in the different grades may thus be compared with the standards for the respective grades.

TABLE XIV

Scores Made By Eleven-Year-Old Pupils of Certain Mill Schools of North Carolina on the Thorndike-McCall Reading Scale Distributed by Grades

Scores	Grade I	Grade II	Grade III	Grade IV	Grade V	Grade VI	Grade VII	Grade VIII	Total
22................	4	14	12	2	....	....	....	....	32
24................	1	4	8	1	....	....	....	....	14
26................	....	3	12	2	....	....	....	....	17
27................	....	1	2	1	....	....	....	....	4
28................	....	2	5	1	....	....	....	....	8
28.5..............	....	....	2	2	....	....	....	....	4
29................	....	2	6	4	....	....	....	....	12
30................	....	1	7	1	....	....	1	....	10
31................	....	1	2	5	....	....	....	....	8
31.5..............	....	2	7	6	....	....	....	....	15
32................	....	....	5	6	2	....	....	....	13
33................	....	1	2	8	2	....	....	....	13
34................	....	....	4	11	6	....	....	....	21
35................	....	....	3	8	3	....	....	....	14
36................	....	1	1	8	3	....	....	....	13
37................	....	....	....	8	8	....	....	....	16
38................	....	....	1	8	9	1	....	....	19
40................	....	....	3	7	15	2	....	....	27
41................	....	1	1	6	14	1	....	....	23
43................	....	....	2	3	12	8	....	....	25
45................	....	....	1	7	7	10	....	....	25
47................	....	....	....	6	11	5	....	....	22
49................	....	....	....	4	7	9	....	....	20
51................	....	....	....	....	3	3	1	....	7
53................	....	....	....	....	7	4	....	....	11
55................	....	....	1	1	2	2	1	....	7
57................	....	....	....	....	....	....	1	....	1
59................	....	....	....	....	....	1	1	....	2
61................	....	....	....	....	....	2	1	1	4
65................	....	....	....	....	....	1	....	....	1
69................	....	....	....	....	....	....	·1	....	1
Total..............	5	33	87	116	111	49	7	1	409
Median............	22.3	25.2	29.4	35.5	42	48	57	61	37.7
Standard for Time of Test..........	....	26	31.2	38.0	42.8	48.9	54.6	58.7	....

Standard Score for Eleven-Year-Old Pupils........................ 45.0

TABLE XV
SCORES MADE ON THORNDIKE-McCALL READING SCALE BY SEVENTH-GRADE
PUPILS OF THE MILL SCHOOLS TESTED

Scores	School No. 1	School No. 2	School No. 3	School No. 5	School No. 6	School No. 8	Total
22......	....	....	....	....	....	....	....
24......	....	....	....	....	....	....	....
26......	1	....	....	....	....	....	1
28......	....	....	....	....	....	....	....
28.5.....	....	....	....	....	....	....	....
29......	....	....	....	....	....	....	....
30......	....	1	....	....	....	....	1
31......	....	....	....	....	....	....	....
31.5.....	....	....	....	....	....	....	....
32......	....	....	....	....	....	....	....
33......	....	....	....	1	....	....	1
34......	....	....	....	....	....	....	....
35......	....	....	....	....	....	....	....
36......	....	1	....	2	....	....	3
37......	....	1	....	....	....	....	1
38......	....	1	....	....	....	....	1
40......	....	3	2	....	....	....	5
41......	1	3	2	2	....	1	9
43......	1	5	2	1	....	2	11
45......	....	5	5	1	2	2	15
47......	2	12	2	....	5	1	22
49......	1	8	1	3	2	3	18
51......	3	6	2	1	3	2	17
53......	1	10	1	....	....	2	14
55......	2	4	1	3	....	4	14
57......	1	2	....	2	1	1	7
59......	....	7	....	1	....	2	10
61......	3	1	1	1	....	....	6
65......	....	2	....	....	....	....	2
69......	1	1	....	....	....	....	2
Total....	17	73	19	18	13	20	160
Median..	52.8	50.1	46	50.3	47.8	52	50.1

Standard Score for the End of the Lower Seventh Grade......... 56.0
Standard for the End of the Upper Sixth Grade................... 53.7

The tabulation of the scores of the seventh-grade pupils in the same test is shown in Table XV. The distribution is on the basis of pupils and schools.

The Thorndike-McCall Scale was given the last week of October. It is thought best in estimating the standing of the grades to compare the median of the grade with the normal median at the end of the preceding as well as with the norm at the end of the grade tested. The median score of the seventh-grade pupils was 50.1. The standard median for the end of the upper sixth grade is 53.7, that for the end of the lower seventh, 56.0. About seven weeks of school had elapsed from the beginning of the term to the giving of the tests, or a little more than one-third of the first half of the school year. The just standard with which to compare the results in the seventh grade is that which may be obtained by adding one-third of the difference between the norm for the end of the upper sixth grade and that of the end of the upper seventh to the norm for the end of the upper sixth grade. The result is 54.5. The seventh-grade pupils of the mill schools are nearer the standard in reading than they are in that of general intelligence, but not so near as they are to the standard in arithmetic.

The eleven-year-old pupils compare, as in arithmetic, much more favorably with the standards of the grade in which they are respectively distributed than they do with the standard for the eleven-year-old group. The median score of the group of eleven-year-old children is 37.7; the standard median for this group is 45. The standards with which the work of the children in the respective grades are compared were obtained by the same method as was that of the seventh grade; namely, by adding one-third of the difference between the standard for the end of the upper grade next preceding and that for the end of the actual grade to the standard for the end of the upper grade next preceding. The median score of the eleven-year-old pupils in the third grade is 29.4; the standard for the grade is 31.2. The eleven-year-old children of the fourth grade fell 2.5 points below the standard; those of the fifth grade .8 points below; those of the sixth grade .9 below; and those of the seventh grade were 2.4 points above the standard for that grade. Measured by grade standards the children of eleven years of age in the mill schools are practically up to standard,—unfamiliarity with the tests being considered.

According to a comparison of the age standards for the group, the median for the group tested falls 7.3 points below standard.

In order that the variation in results of the different tests with respect to the difference in standing by using the age or grade standard as the basis of comparison may be observed, Table XVI is given.

TABLE XVI

COMPARISON OF THE STANDING OF 409 ELEVEN-YEAR-OLD PUPILS IN GENERAL INTELLIGENCE, ARITHMETIC, AND READING, AS ESTIMATED BY AGE STANDARDS AND THE STANDARDS OF THE RESPECTIVE GRADES IN WHICH THE CHILDREN ARE DISTRIBUTED

	Medians						
	Grade III	Grade IV	Grade V	Grade VI	Grade VII	Grade VIII	Eleven-Year-Old Pupils
Mill Children	28	55	71.5	90.5	131.2	151	56
National Intelligence, Scale B, Form I Standard.	......	77	96	110	120	138	96
Mill Children......	5.1	13.2	17.6	21	23	23	13.6
Woody-McCall Mixed Fundamentals Standard............	6.8	13.1	17.8	22.5	25.9	27.8	22.6
Mill Children......	29.4	35.3	42	48	57	61	37.7
Thorndike-McCall Reading Standard............	31.2	38	42.8	48.9	54.6	58.7	45

Based on this summary of results and the record of the seventh-grade pupils tested, the conclusion is that the mill children are farther below standard in general intelligence than in either arithmetic or reading achievement. The deficiencies of mill schools and the mill environment affect the opportunities of children to obtain general information more disastrously than they affect achievements in the other accomplishments tested. Pupils with very low intelligence quotients do not fall much below the standards of their respective grades in arithmetical and reading achievements. The accelerated pupils, while considerably above the norms of their respective grades in general intelligence and reading, fall below the standard norms of these grades in arithmetic. The average of the pupils tested in the seventh grade is 13.8 years, and 120 of the 162 pupils are over-age. The median intelligence quotient of the pupils in this grade is 86.5. Yet the achievement in arithmetic fundamentals is practically up to the standard. Retarded children of low intelligence quotients in this instance also are capable of coming up to standard in the fundamentals of arithmetic.

The achievements of mill children based on grade norms would seem to be fairly satisfactory. But the children have not attained the advancement which other children of their age appear to have reached as ascertained by the norms for the age-grades. The norms for the age-groups, as has been indicated elsewhere, are likely to be somewhat too high as a result of not including a due proportion of children of inferior attainment. The results of this test give indication but not proof of this.

The eleven-year-old and seventh-grade pupils have attained, by training, achievement in the studies tested which almost reaches the accepted standards for grades. But this training has failed to bring up in a proportionate degree the scores in the general intelligence test. This leaves the low standing in general intelligence of mill children, as revealed by scores, intelligence quotients, and percentile rankings, to be explained by a relatively lower mental capacity on the part of the mill children and by the lack of stimulating influence in the mill schools and a mill environment. The exact degree to which each factor is responsible for this low standing in general intelligence can not with present facilities be accurately measured. Nothing can be done by the schools to improve this condition insofar as results are due to the first factor; but improvement in school and social opportunities will help ameliorate what is due to the second factor.

CHAPTER IV

EDUCATIONAL OPPORTUNITIES OF MILL CHILDREN

THE course of study in the public schools of North Carolina is eleven years in length. There are usually seven grades for the elementary work and four for that of the high school. Three cities of the state have opportunities for twelve years of work, one of which is Roanoke Rapids with a mill school. Children who live outside a district maintaining a high school may have tuition paid by the county for six months of the year. For the remainder of the term the children must pay their own tuition.[21] In the case of children living just without the city school districts, this would mean a payment of tuition for a term of three months. Children in Erlanger and Caroleen do not have to pay tuition to attend high school, as the schools are included in a special high school district. The children of White Oak, Proximity and Revolution in Guilford County may have free high school tuition if they attend rural high schools in the county but must pay tuition to attend the high school in the city of Greensboro; however, the mills are within the corporate limits of the city. All other children living in seven-, eight-, nine- or ten-grade schools are required to pay tuition for the term beyond six months for each year that they attend high school.

Data (shown in Table XVII) with respect to the number of grades provided were secured from 115 mill schools. The number of children attending the schools of the different groups is given on the basis of 109 schools.

There are 441 pupils living in mill school districts who in order to receive a high school education must pay tuition for the length of term beyond six months for five years; 11,659 for four years; 316 for three years; 2,628 for two years; and 417 for one year. In addition, more than one-half of these children would have to

---

[21] The Public School Law of North Carolina, Codification of 1923, p. 64, Sec. 241.

TABLE XVII

NUMBER OF CHILDREN ENROLLED IN DIFFERENT TYPES OF MILL SCHOOLS

Number of Grades in School	Number of Schools	Number of Pupils
Eleven	35	19,378
Ten	2	417
Nine	8	2,628
Eight	2	316
Seven	66	12,258
Six	2	441
Total	115	

provide transportation to high school or pay board. In all, 15,245 children are limited in opportunities for a high school education by living in mill school districts.

The effect of different types of mill schools on high school opportunities and probabilities of attendance beyond the compulsory age limit will be estimated from age-grade data in the following tables. Tables of mill schools will be given. In addition, other data will be given for the purpose of comparison. In mill schools which do not offer eleven years of work, the data in regard to high school attendance elsewhere of children residing in mill school districts were secured. This was obtained from the principals of mill schools and checked by reports from principals of the high school where the mill children attended. In cases where accurate data were not obtainable, the schools are not included in the report.

In case of mill schools which had a high school department, tuition pupils were not included but only those living within the school district.

For the purpose of comparison, the age-grade distribution of the special-chartered schools of North Carolina was secured. These systems included those villages, towns and cities which are without the supervision of the county superintendents. These school systems vary in enrollment from 217 to 11,996 each. There are in each of these school systems eleven grades.

The distribution in the rural districts is also included for purposes of comparison. The rural schools are the schools under direct county supervision and include all types and sizes of rural schools in North Carolina.

The age-grade distribution of the City of Greensboro is included for the purpose of comparing the school advantages of children just without the city school district with those of the children within the city school district. There are 1,772 children within

TABLE XVIII

ENROLLMENT BY AGE AND GRADE IN SPECIAL CHARTER SCHOOL OF NORTH CAROLINA

Age	Grade I	Grade II	Grade III	Grade IV	Grade V	Grade VI	Grade VII	Grade VIII	Grade IX	Grade X	Grade XI	Total
6	10,671	517	25	1	.....	.....	.....	.....	.....	.....	.....	11,214
7	5,894	6,066	873	29	2	.....	.....	.....	.....	.....	.....	12,864
8	2,559	4,776	5,242	861	70	.....	.....	.....	.....	.....	.....	13,508
9	1,101	2,397	4,532	4,477	695	28	2	.....	.....	.....	.....	13,232
10	608	1,266	2,660	4,195	3,798	643	41	.....	.....	.....	.....	13,211
11	270	642	1,425	2,665	3,646	2,850	635	42	3	.....	.....	12,178
12	167	383	957	1,785	2,480	3,059	2,607	608	30	1	.....	12,077
13	81	250	529	1,091	1,688	2,094	2,687	2,343	429	26	.....	11,218
14	23	78	226	510	853	1,327	2,036	2,830	1,730	315	21	9,948
15	7	14	37	148	287	761	1,325	2,287	2,196	1,320	219	8,601
16	.....	6	12	48	118	253	610	1,322	1,540	1,694	1,043	6,646
17	1	.....	2	4	43	84	205	610	860	1,195	1,378	4,382
18	.....	.....	.....	5	5	29	69	255	487	666	989	2,505
19	.....	.....	.....	5	4	6	30	77	139	299	487	1,047
20	.....	.....	.....	.....	3	1	7	68	53	95	182	409
21 and Over	.....	.....	.....	.....	1	1	3	18	28	46	86	183
Total	21,382	16,395	16,520	15,824	13,693	11,136	10,257	10,460	7,495	7,657	4,404	133,223
Per Cent in Each Grade	16.	12.3	12.4	11.9	10.3	8.4	7.7	7.9	5.6	4.2	3.3	

TABLE XIX

ENROLLMENT BY AGE AND GRADE OF CHILDREN IN THE RURAL SCHOOLS OF NORTH CAROLINA

Age	Grade I	Grade II	Grade III	Grade IV	Grade V	Grade VI	Grade VII	Grade VIII	Grade IX	Grade X	Grade XI	Total
6	37,472	2,422	110	15	.....	.....	.....	.....	.....	.....	.....	40,019
7	26,623	13,179	1,884	199	3	5	.....	.....	.....	.....	.....	41,893
8	14,650	14,631	11,012	2,457	221	4	.....	.....	.....	.....	.....	42,975
9	7,512	10,407	13,355	8,519	1,708	145	2	.....	.....	.....	.....	41,648
10	4,046	6,773	10,861	11,608	7,176	1,295	104	3	.....	.....	.....	41,866
11	2,074	3,992	7,439	10,420	10,053	5,451	905	75	5	6	.....	40,420
12	1,196	2,396	4,965	8,373	9,051	7,206	3,949	589	53	3	.....	37,781
13	613	1,262	3,120	5,547	7,467	7,343	6,085	1,968	335	30	.....	33,770
14	332	630	1,549	3,609	5,051	6,640	7,182	3,351	1,603	225	24	30,196
15	104	243	605	1,555	2,766	4,080	6,308	3,854	2,201	913	141	22,770
16	42	55	236	648	1,121	2,296	4,307	3,092	2,384	1,611	731	16,523
17	23	30	63	208	464	1,070	2,397	2,126	1,927	1,659	1,070	11,037
18	4	10	26	82	206	457	1,125	1,248	1,285	1,258	1,054	6,855
19	3	5	5	23	43	151	500	600	675	747	708	3,460
20	1	1	1	15	33	46	203	299	290	379	478	1,746
21	.....	1	.....	1	6	11	36	96	154	186	255	746
Total	94,695	36,037	55,231	53,279	45,369	36,200	33,203	17,301	10,912	7,017	4,461	413,705
Per Cent in Each Grade	22.9	13.5	13.4	12.9	11.0	8.7	8.0	4.2	2.6	1.7	1.1	

the corporate limits of Greensboro enrolled in 'three mill schools with seven grades in the organization. These children are included in the age-grade distribution of the seven-grade systems. By this comparison, school advantages which the mill children living just outside of the special-chartered districts might enjoy in case they were not segregated into mill schools are evident. There are in all, with five such schools not reporting, 7,405 children in mill schools without a special-chartered school district, who are forced to attend mill schools rather than to be included within the city school systems.

TABLE XX

Enrollment by Age and Grade in the Schools of Greensboro, Which Includes in its Corporate Limits but without its School District, Three Large Mill Schools

Age	Grade I	Grade II	Grade III	Grade IV	Grade V	Grade VI	Grade VII	Grade VIII	Grade IX	Grade X	Grade XI	Tota
6	218	8	1	.....	.....	.....	.....	.....	.....	.....	.....	227
7	149	170	31	.....	.....	.....	.....	.....	.....	.....	.....	350
8	36	125	131	14	.....	.....	.....	.....	.....	.....	.....	306
9	10	47	135	132	19	.....	.....	.....	.....	.....	.....	343
10	2	15	63	132	103	22	.....	.....	.....	.....	.....	337
11	.....	5	28	61	90	107	10	2	.....	.....	.....	313
12	.....	2	16	29	56	110	81	9	1	.....	.....	304
13	1	2	2	8	30	65	111	62	11	2	.....	294
14	.....	.....	3	3	10	19	59	112	67	11	2	286
15	.....	.....	.....	.....	3	14	28	75	76	48	2	246
16	.....	.....	1	.....	.....	8	22	31	57	74	33	227
17	.....	.....	.....	.....	.....	.....	3	11	43	51	72	180
18	.....	.....	.....	.....	.....	.....	2	7	15	21	60	105
19	.....	.....	.....	.....	.....	.....	.....	3	6	4	17	30
20	.....	.....	.....	.....	.....	.....	.....	1	2	2	1	6
Total	416	374	411	380	311	345	321	311	278	213	187	3,554
Per Cent in Each Grade	11.8	10.5	11.6	10.7	8.8	9.7	9.1	8.7	7.8	6	5.3	

The age-grade distribution of mill children is included under three separate types; those of eleven, nine and seven grades. The enclosed map of North Carolina indicates the location of the schools within the distribution. Included in the distribution, are all the schools from which accurate information could be obtained. The total enrollment in the mill schools of North Carolina, excluding nine small schools from which data could not be secured is 36,222. The enrollment from the schools excluded would raise the total about 1,300 to 1,500. The number of children included in the age-grade distribution is 18,925, or about one-half of the total number of children enrolled. There are sixteen mill schools of the thirty-one eleven-grade systems included in the distribution for this type of school. The schools included are Spray, Kannapolis, Haw River, Cliffside, Spindale, Duke, Gibsonville, East Flat Rock, Altamahaw-Ossipee, Cooleemee, Hope Mills, West Durham, Roanoke Rapids, Ranlo, Lowel and Dallas.

TABLE XXI

Age-Grade Distribution of Children in Sixteen Mill Schools With Eleven Grades in the System

Age	Grade I	Grade II	Grade III	Grade IV	Grade V	Grade VI	Grade VII	Grade VIII	Grade IX	Grade X	Grade XI	Total
5	141	6	....	....	....	....	....	....	....	....	....	147
6	848	96	6	....	....	....	....	....	....	....	....	950
7	616	404	78	11	....	....	....	....	....	....	....	1,109
8	364	404	319	97	3	....	....	....	....	....	....	1,187
9	168	263	402	262	67	2	....	....	....	....	....	1,164
10	75	166	279	328	195	51	5	1	....	....	....	1,110
11	39	80	175	292	274	162	35	5	....	....	....	1,062
12	29	49	130	245	233	227	105	27	7	....	....	1,052
13	6	36	57	134	189	177	147	103	24	1	....	874
14	6	2	15	45	83	123	128	118	69	20	....	609
15	....	....	5	11	38	59	93	121	92	69	17	505
16	....	....	....	3	15	19	38	71	82	71	56	355
17	....	....	....	1	4	6	16	33	41	57	63	221
18	....	....	....	....	1	....	6	9	22	37	49	124
19	....	....	....	....	....	....	2	7	7	23	17	56
20	....	....	....	....	....	....	....	3	3	6	14	26
21	....	....	....	....	....	....	....	6	1	4	5	16
21 —	....	....	....	....	....	....	....	....	....	3	5	8
Total	2,292	1,506	1,466	1,429	1,112	826	575	504	348	291	226	10,575
Per Cent in Each Grade	21.7	14.3	13.9	13.5	10.5	7.8	5.4	4.8	3.3	2.7	2.1	

The nine-grade systems included in Table XXI are Flint Grove, Cramerton, Whitnel, North Charlotte and Hoskins. There are eight North Carolina mill schools which have nine-grade systems. The total number of pupils enrolled in some tenth and eleventh grades are included. It was not possible to get accurate data concerning their age, so the total only is included. The pupils included in the tenth and eleventh grades of this table are those with parents living within the mill school districts.

In the age-grade distribution of the children of seven-grade systems twenty-two of the sixty-six mill schools in this class are included. There are included, however, 6,452 pupils of the 12,258 enrolled in such schools. The total high school attendance is reported by grades but not by age. The pupils included are those with parents living within the mill school districts. The following schools are included in the table: Nokomis, Hartsell, Brown-

Norcutt, Rowan, Wicassett-Efird, Yadkin, Saxapahaw, Rohanen, Glenwood, Worthville, North Belmont, Erlanger, Capelsie, Icemorlee, Lynn, Glen Raven, Hanes, East Lumberton, Jinnings, Revolution, Proximity and White Oak.

A comparison of the percentage of pupils attending schools in the different grades and especially in high schools will be made to determine the effect of mill schools and opportunities for employment in mills on the per cent of pupils attending high schools.

In Table XXV the number attending high schools from the different types of schools is compared with the number enrolled in nine-, ten-, eleven- and twelve-year-old groups of the respective systems. A perfect high school attendance would approximate 100 per cent of this total. This comparison reveals differences of high school opportunity similar to that based on total enrollment. The eleven-grade systems of mill schools have 12.9 per cent of their enrollment in high school compared to 7.5 per cent for the nine-grade systems and 3.2 per cent for the seven-grade systems. This shows that the high school enrollment of mill children is commensurate with their high school opportunities. It

TABLE XXII

Age-Grade Distribution of Children in Five Mill Schools With Nine Grades in the System. Those in Some Tenth and Eleventh-Grade Given in Total Only

Age	Grade I	Grade II	Grade III	Grade IV	Grade V	Grade VI	Grade VII	Grade VIII	Grade IX	Grade X	Grade XI	Total
5	13											13
6	222	5										227
7	122	93	10	4								229
8	53	87	43	9								192
9	22	57	66	58	3							206
10	10	32	69	54	38							203
11	6	20	29	44	57	18	6	5				185
12	3	8	28	28	53	48	17	5				190
13	2	9	7	29	32	65	28	20				192
14	1		8	15	14	27	34	17	10			126
15			1	4	4	17	14	10	12			62
16			1			3	5	9	13			31
17							1	2	3			6
18									4			4
19									2			2
20												
Total Including Those in Other High Schools	454	311	262	245	201	178	105	68	44	22	8	1,868
												30
												1,898
Per Cent in Each Grade	23.9	16.4	13.8	12.9	10.6	9.4	5.5	3.6	2.3	1.2	.4	

TABLE XXIII

AGE-GRADE DISTRIBUTION IN TWENTY-TWO MILL SCHOOLS WITH SEVEN GRADES IN THE SYSTEM. THOSE ENROLLED IN SOME EIGHTH, NINTH, TENTH, OR ELEVENTH GRADE GIVEN IN TOTAL ONLY

Age	Grade I	Grade II	Grade III	Grade IV	Grade V	Grade VI	Grade VII	Grade VIII	Grade IX	Grade X	Grade XI	Total
5	4	....	....	....	....	....	....	....	....	....	....	4
6	715	7	....	....	....	....	....	....	....	....	....	722
7	524	212	6	1	....	....	....	....	....	....	....	743
8	275	321	136	12	....	....	....	....	....	....	....	744
9	161	251	218	124	19	1	....	....	....	....	....	774
10	71	157	266	211	83	7	....	....	....	....	....	795
11	30	67	173	210	153	68	4	....	....	....	....	705
12	20	49	114	191	189	124	42	....	....	....	....	729
13	6	22	89	97	151	120	94	....	....	....	....	579
14	2	4	19	35	63	75	91	....	....	....	....	289
15	....	....	4	11	22	30	37	....	....	....	....	104
16	....	....	....	....	5	7	15	....	....	....	....	27
17	....	....	....	1	....	3	4	....	....	....	....	8
18	....	....	....	....	1	3	2	....	....	....	....	6
19	....	....	....	....	....	1	3	....	....	....	....	4
20	....	....	....	....	....	....	....	....	....	....	....	....
Total	808	1,090	1,023	895	686	439	292	89	54	48	28	6,233
Including Those in High Schools	....	....	....	....	....	....	....	....	....	....	....	219
												6,452
Per Cent in Each Grade	28.2	16.9	15.9	13.9	10.6	6.8	4.5	1.3	.8	.7	.4	

TABLE XXIV

COMPARING DIFFERENT TYPES OF MILL SCHOOLS WITH ONE ANOTHER AND WITH GREENSBORO, SPECIAL-CHARTERED SCHOOLS AND RURAL SCHOOLS IN PERCENTAGE OF ENROLLMENT IN EACH GRADE

School System	Percentage											Per Cent of High School Enrollment
	Grade I	Grade II	Grade III	Grade IV	Grade V	Grade VI	Grade VII	Grade VIII	Grade IX	Grade X	Grade XI	
Greensboro	11.8	10.5	11.6	10.7	8.8	9.7	9.1	8.7	7.8	6	5.3	28.4
Special Chartered Schools	16.	12.3	12.4	11.9	10.3	8.4	7.7	7.9	5.6	4.2	3.3	21.0
Rural Schools	22.9	13.5	13.4	12.9	11.0	8.7	8.0	4.2	2.6	1.7	1.1	9.6
Eleven-Grade Mill Schools	21.7	14.3	13.9	13.5	10.5	7.8	5.4	4.8	3.3	2.7	2.1	12.9
Nine-Grade Mill Schools	23.9	16.4	13.8	12.9	10.6	9.4	5.5	3.6	2.3	1.2	.4	7.5
Seven-Grade Mill Schools	28.2	16.9	15.9	13.9	10.6	6.8	4.5	1.3	.8	.7	.4	3.2

TABLE XXV

COMPARING DIFFERENT TYPES OF MILL SCHOOLS WITH ONE ANOTHER AND WITH GREENSBORO, SPECIAL-CHARTERED SCHOOLS AND RURAL SCHOOLS IN THE PERCENTAGE OF THE HIGH SCHOOL ENROLLMENT OF THE NUMBER IN THE FOUR AGE-GROUPS

School Systems	Number in Four Age-Groups	Pupils in High School	Percentage
Greensboro..............	1,289	989	77
Special-Chartered Schools..	51,204	30,006	58.6
Rural Schools	163,792	39,691	24.2
Eleven-Grade Mill Schools.	4,488	1,369	30.5
Nine-Grade Mill Schools ..	800	132	16.5
Seven-Grade Mill Schools..	2,968	219	7.0

reveals the fact that many more children in the seven-grade and nine-grade systems are prevented from getting a high school education by lack of funds with which to pay tuition, board or transportation. Children living in such mill school districts are penalized educationally. It is probable, that, lacking high school opportunity, they are also more likely to seek employment in the mills at an early age.

The presence of mills in the community is in itself a constant temptation to children to leave school before entering or completing high school. This is indicated by the enrollment in high school of the eleven-grade mill school systems being proportionately less than that of the high schools in special-chartered districts and cities. Such percentage of enrollment in the high schools of the eleven-grade mill schools is compared to that of the special-chartered districts in Greensboro.

But the extent of the lack of high school educational advantages of children in the nine-grade and seven-grade systems is alarming. Even the children of the rural districts of North Carolina, which are very inadequately supplied with high schools, have a larger percentage of children enrolled in high school than either of these types of mill schools. As a rule the children of mill-workers would have had three times as much chance for a high school education had the father remained in the rural districts rather than moved to a mill village which maintains schools of only seven grades.

The percentage of children of the thirteen- and fourteen-year-old groups enrolled in school is important in view of the North

Carolina Compulsory Attendance and Child Labor Laws. All children between seven and fourteen years of age are required to attend school. Children may enter employment for sixty hours a week at fourteen years of age.[22]

To determine the proportion of children of thirteen and fourteen years of age in school, the standard age-group was obtained by finding the average number of children enrolled in the eight-, nine-, ten-, eleven- and twelve-year-old groups of each system. The percentage of pupils of thirteen and fourteen years of age enrolled in school was determined upon the basis of this average. The result is given for each type of mill school and for the systems used as a basis of comparison.

That the Compulsory Attendance Law is not well enforced in the mill schools, as a whole, is evident. A little more than twenty per cent of the thirteen-year-old children in mill districts is not enrolled. The proportion of this group which is not enrolled is

TABLE XXVI

Number and Percentage of Children of Thirteen and Fourteen Years of Age Enrolled in Mill Schools of Eleven Grades. Percentage is Based on Average Enrollment of Children of Eight, Nine, Ten, Eleven and Twelve Years of Age

School	Average Enrollment in the Five Age-Groups	Thirteen-Year-Old Children		Fourteen-Year-Old Children	
		Number Enrolled	Per Cent Enrolled	Number Enrolled	Per Cent Enrolled
Kannapolis............	171	85	49.1	57	33.3
Spray................	101	33	32.6	24	23.8
Haw River............	33	43	130.3	25	75.5
Cliffside.............	76	62	81.6	44	57.8
Spindale.............	55	39	72.7	38	70.9
Duke................	61	54	88.5	28	45.9
Gibsonville...........	40	43	107.5	31	77.5
East Flat Rock.......	28	21	75	24	85.7
Altamahaw-Ossipee....	24	27	112.5	15	62.5
Cooleemee...........	74	74	100	64	86.5
Hope Mills...........	39	32	82.1	27	69.2
West Durham.........	132	132	100	83	62.8
Roanoke Rapids......	136	129	94.8	85	62.5
Ranlo...............	63	54	85.7	22	34.9
Lowell...............	47	31	65.9	27	57.4
Dallas...............	42	25	59.5	29	69
Total............	1,122	883	78.7	613	54.6

[22] The Public School Law of North Carolina, Codification of 1923, p. 94, Sec. 247.

TABLE XXVII

NUMBER AND PERCENTAGE OF CHILDREN OF THIRTEEN AND FOURTEEN YEARS
OF AGE ENROLLED IN MILL SCHOOLS OF NINE GRADES. PERCENTAGE IS
BASED ON THE AVERAGE ENROLLMENT OF CHILDREN OF EIGHT, NINE, TEN
AND ELEVEN YEARS OF AGE

School	Average Enrollment in the Five Age-Groups	Thirteen-Year-Old Children		Fourteen-Year-Old Children	
		Number Enrolled	Per Cent Enrolled	Number Enrolled	Per Cent Enrolled
Flint Grove..........	38	36	97.4	19	50
Cramerton............	55	53	96.4	30	54.5
Whitnel.............	26	25	96.2	21	80.8
North Charlotte......	40	31	77.5	22	54
Hoskins.............	41	52	126.8	34	82.9
Total..........	200	197	98.5	126	63.0

TABLE XXVIII

NUMBER AND PERCENTAGE OF CHILDREN OF THIRTEEN AND FOURTEEN YEARS
OF AGE ENROLLED IN DIFFERENT MILL SCHOOLS OF SEVEN GRADES. PER-
CENTAGE IS BASED ON AVERAGE ENROLLMENT OF CHILDREN OF EIGHT, NINE,
TEN, ELEVEN AND TWELVE YEARS OF AGE

School	Average Enrollment in the Five Age-Groups	Thirteen-Year-Old Children		Fourteen-Year-Old Children	
		Number Enrolled	Per Cent Enrolled	Number Enrolled	Per Cent Enrolled
Wicassett-Efird.......	139	103	74.1	37	26.6
White Oak...........	99	68	68.6	46	46.5
Rohanen.............	76	57	75	28	36.8
East Lumberton......	21	16	76.2	11	52.4
Icemorlee...........	14	8	57.1	6	42.9
Hartsell............	37	26	70.3	17	46
Nokomis.............	23	20	87	8	34.8
Brown-Norcutt.......	26	13	50	3	1.2
Rowan..............	6	2	33.3	3	50
Yadkin.............	5	3	60	4	80
Saxapahaw..........	15	16	101.6	14	93.3
Glenwood...........	9	6	66.7	5	55.5
Worthville..........	11	10	90.9	9	81.8
North Belmont.......	50	39	78	17	34
Erlanger............	31	20	64.5	17	54.8
Capelsie............	8	10	125	1	12.5
Lynn...............	10	9	90	9	90
Glen Raven..........	13	6	46.2	6	46.2
Hanes..............	35	34	97.1	12	34.3
Jennings............	10	2	20	0	0
Revolution..........	44	42	95.5	20	45.5
Proximity...........	60	47	78.3	20	33.3
Total..........	742	547	73.7	273	36.8

TABLE XXIX

NUMBER AND PERCENTAGE OF CHILDREN OF THIRTEEN AND FOURTEEN YEARS
OF AGE IN SCHOOL WHO LIVE IN MILL SCHOOL DISTRICTS OF DIFFERENT
TYPES

School Systems	Average Enrollment in the Five Age-Groups	Thirteen-Year-Old Children		Fourteen-Year-Old Children	
		Number Enrolled	Per Cent Enrolled	Number Enrolled	Per Cent Enrolled
Eleven-Grade Systems	1,122	883	78.7	613	54.6
Nine-Grade Systems	200	197	98.5	126	63
Seven-Grade Systems	742	547	73.7	273	36.8
Rural Schools of North Carolina...............	40,948	33,770	82.5	30,196	73.7
Special-Chartered Schools of North Carolina.........	12,801	11,218	87.7	9,948	77.7
Greensboro..............	321	294	91.3	286	89.1

higher than in rural districts and considerably higher than that in the special-chartered school districts with which it is more justly comparable. There are between 800 and 1,000 children of thirteen years of age living in mill school districts of North Carolina who are illegally out of school. There is only one mill village which employs an attendance officer for a part of the time. Carrboro, in conjunction with Chapel Hill, has an officer employed part of the time for this purpose. In this village, twenty-four children thirteen years of age are enrolled. The number of children thirteen years of age in the village, as gathered from the method used in other cases, is twenty-six. What is done in this one mill village needs to be done and could be done in all. For some reason or other, the authorities of mill schools, as a class, are failing to enforce the compulsory attendance law of the state.

Of the fourteen-year-old group living in mill village districts, 49.8 per cent are enrolled in school. A large majority of principals report that it is a common practice for children to quit school the day they reach fourteen years of age. If we may use an estimate based on the attainments of the thirteen-year-old group, it is plain a large number of mill children will leave school with very low standards of educational attainments. The thirteen-year-old children included in the age-grade distribution are distributed by grades as follows:

First	Second	Third	Fourth	Fifth	Sixth	Seventh	Eighth	Ninth	Tenth	Total
14	56	153	260	372	362	269	123	24	1	1645

From this group will come those who will stop school at fourteen. It will be seen that the standard of educational attainments of the larger number is quite low compared with the desirable minimum standards for· the education of future citizens. There are 855 children or 52 per cent in the fifth grade or below. Fourteen-year-old mill children are leaving, too often, with unusually low educational achievements. The law lacks an educational requirement for the employment of fourteen-year-old children, which is somewhat responsible for the large drain from the schools to the mill at the age of fourteen.

The upper limit of the compulsory attendance law and the lower limit of the child labor law is fourteen years.[22a] No state has a lower age as the upper limit of the compulsory attendance law. Five states only have the same limit. They are Georgia, Mississippi, South Carolina, Texas and Virginia. The number of children between fourteen and sixteen in the cotton mills of North Carolina was, according to the last report, 4,772.[23] The large falling off of the fourteen-year-old children is, thus, largely but not entirely accounted for, as there are 8,228 children in the fourteen- and fifteen-year-old groups in mill districts only. In addition there are several mill schools in city school systems which are not included in this study.

The large number of the fourteen- and fifteen-year-old group of mill children unemployed and also out of school constitutes another phase of the problem of the low standing of mill schools with respect to retaining children of fourteen years and older. The following reasons why these children are not in school, although unemployed, have been given by principals.

First, children often quit school to take temporary employment or fail to hold their jobs. In either case they rarely return to school. Second, in seven-grade school systems, free opportunities for further education are not often provided for children of this age, who have made normal progress through the grades. Third, the attitude of parents and of the mill communities towards educational advantages is often reported as that of indifference.

The failure to hold more than fifty per cent of the fourteen-

[22a] The Public School Law of North Carolina, Codification of 1923, p. 64, Sec. 241.
[23] Records of North Carolina Labor and Printing, Raleigh, North Carolina.

year-old group in school is one of the most serious defects of the mill schools. In this respect the rural schools of North Carolina, as a whole, are almost fifty per cent more efficient. Better results than those now secured should be expected. Recommendations will be made later in this study.

It is to be noted that the nine-grade systems of mill schools surpass both the seven- and eleven-grade systems in ability to hold both thirteen- and fourteen-year-old children. The percentage of the thirteen-year-old pupils in schools is 98.5 per cent of the whole group. The ability of the nine-grade systems to hold this group surpasses that of any other type shown in Table XXIX. None of the schools of this type which reported employed an attendance officer. The facilities and teachers in these schools did not, on the whole, rank as high as those of the eleven-grade group. There is no other factor in which the schools of the nine-grade systems differ essentially from the other type of mill schools. It is evident that the nine-grade organization has succeeded in holding in school more thirteen- and fourteen-year-old children of mill schools than has either of the other two types.

The course of study in the elementary grades of the mill schools as reported in every case met the minimum essentials of the North Carolina state course. The following subjects are those required and those reported as taken in the first seven grades of all schools: reading, writing, language, history, civics, healthy living, arithmetic, spelling and geography. In Table XXX only additions to the above list of subjects will be noted.

TABLE XXX

SUBJECTS INCLUDED IN ELEMENTARY COURSE OF STUDY IN MILL SCHOOLS IN ADDITION TO THE SUBJECTS COMMON TO ALL

Subjects	Seven-Grade Systems	Nine-Grade Systems	Eleven-Grade Systems
Drawing...............	4	2	8
Music.................	2	0	5
Science...............	3	2	6
Physical Education.......	2	0	1
Home Economics........	2	0	2
Agriculture.............	1	1	2
Manual Training........	2	0	0
Latin.................	0	1	0
No. of Schools Reporting	26	5	16

From so few cases, not many definite conclusions can be drawn. But it would seem very likely that the addition of a high school to a mill school system sometimes has the effect of adding to the course of study in the elementary grades. At least the eleven- and nine-grade mill school systems have, as a rule, a somewhat richer course of study in the elementary grades than do those of the seven-grade systems. There is much to be desired in the way of an enriched course of study for all mill schools.

It was ascertained from questionnaires given to the seventh-grade children tested that the homes of the mill children are, in the large majority of cases, deficient in the quality and quantity of reading material contained therein. The reading material needed for the growth and development of mill children must be supplied, then, by the village or the school unless facilities for obtaining information and developing reading tastes and interests are entirely neglected. There is a supreme need in mill villages for a wealth of reading material. From principals of schools were secured data in regard to the community and school libraries in the case of 47 mills schools. There were four mill villages of this number which had a community library or reading room. They were Duke, Proximity, Spray and White Oak. Each of these communities had in addition a school library.

Table XXXI gives the estimated number of volumes in the mill school libraries distributed in accordance with the number of grades for each school. Each separate number is that of some school.

TABLE XXXI
NUMBER OF BOOKS IN MILL SCHOOLS

Eleven-Grade Systems...700, 300, 300, 1000, 146, 300, 400, 400, 650, 600, 700, 425, 300, 300, 345, 200

Nine-Grade Systems.....112, 400, 111, 65, 250

Seven-Grade Systems....15, 0, 70, 785, 34, 25, 280, 0, 30, 108, 250, 131, 0, 753, 0, 40, 0, 150, 0, 500, 400, 0, 100, 50, 50

(Number of schools reporting 47)

The reading facilities of mill villages and mill schools are quite limited. There are seven-grade mill schools which have not a book in addition to the text books. Five other schools have fifty or fewer. The library conditions in mill schools are generally worse than appear in the table as the schools reporting include most of the better mill schools and comparatively few of the poorer ones.

It will be noticed that the eleven-grade systems have in every instance, except one, a library of 300 volumes or more. It will be noted also that 300 is the number which appears most frequently. The reason is that high school regulations of North Carolina require as a minimum a library of 300 volumes. In only one instance is a library for elementary grades specified in addition to the high school library.

The conclusion is that with rare exceptions, the reading material available to children of mill schools, especially to those in the elementary grades, is very meager.

By North Carolina certification regulations, the teachers who have as much as 60 semester hours of work in a normal school or college, in addition to high school graduation and including at least six semester hours of professional work, are given primary, grammar-grade or high school certificates. Those below this standard are given lower certificates. A rough comparison of the training of the teachers in the different types of mill schools in accordance with the number of grades in the systems may be made on this basis. There are 314 teachers in the mill schools concerning whom certification facts were available. They were distributed among the different types of schools as indicated in the table below:

TABLE XXXII

COMPARISON OF SEVEN-, NINE-, AND ELEVEN-GRADE SYSTEMS IN RESPECT
TO THE TRAINING OF TEACHERS

School Systems	Teachers with Primary, Grammar Grade, or High School Certificates	Teachers with Lower Certificates	Per Cent of Number Holding Higher Certificates
Eleven-Grade........	94	34	73.4
Nine-Grade.........	32	12	72.7
Seven-Grade........	66	76	46.5
Total..........	192	122	61.2

As a whole, the mill schools of North Carolina employ fewer teachers of higher training than do the special-chartered districts, the percentage of the whole being 61.2 per cent and 87.34 per cent respectively. Even the eleven-grade systems fall below the special-chartered districts by 13.9 per cent. The seven-grade systems fall below the average of the state. Mill children do not have teachers as well trained as the children who attend the special-chartered schools. The fact of having eleven or nine grades increases the percentage of better trained teachers by more than one-half.

The percentages of teachers holding higher certificates in the schools used for comparison are as follows:

TABLE XXXIII
PER CENT OF WHITE TEACHERS HOLDING HIGHER CERTIFICATES

Rural Schools of North Carolina	34.25
Special-Chartered Schools of North Carolina	87.34
City of Greensboro	100.00
All of North Carolina	47.34

Those mill schools which offer a longer course of study hold a greater proportion of thirteen- and fourteen-year-old children in school, have richer curricula in the grades, better libraries, better teachers and they also have a larger proportion of the total enrollment receiving the benefit of a high school education.

As a whole, the proportion of the mill school children attending some high school is smaller than that of the rural children. In the eleven-grade systems of mill schools, 12.9 per cent of the children are enrolled in some high school; in the nine-grade systems, 7.5 per cent; in the seven-grade systems, 3.2 per cent.

If the average enrollment of children eight, nine, ten, eleven and twelve years of age be considered, there is 80 per cent of the thirteen-year-old group of mill children in school and 49.8 per cent of the fourteen-year-old group.

The upper age limit of the compulsory attendance law and the lower one of the child labor law is fourteen in North Carolina. Only five other states have as low a limit. There is no educational requirement in either law.

Only one mill school district has a part-time attendance officer.

The nine-grade mill school systems retain on an average 97.5 per cent of their thirteen-year-old children in school.

Only four mill villages have a community library or reading room. Seven out of 46 mill schools reporting had no books in the school other than texts. School libraries in mill schools are grossly under-supplied with respect to reading material of any sort, especially that for elementary children.

In every item of comparison, mill schools fall far below the special-chartered schools of North Carolina, with which they are justly comparable. The educational opportunities of mill children are much inferior to those of the children living in special-chartered school districts. Opportunities can be equalized if mill school districts contribute to the support of schools to the same extent as the special-chartered districts, and if the local control is made more democratic.

CHAPTER V

RECOMMENDATIONS

BASED on the findings of previous chapters, recommendations for the improvement of educational opportunities and facilities of mill children will be made along three lines, legislative, social and political, and educational. Before an adequate educational program can be reasonably successful certain changes must be made in the laws of the State of North Carolina and certain depressive social tendencies must be corrected by the force of public opinion.

LEGISLATIVE

1. The ownership of buildings by mill companies gives too much potential control to the owners of the mill whose economic interests conflict with the educational interests of the children. It has been shown that in every case where both the extra term is paid for by subsidy and the building owned by the mill companies, only seven years of school work is provided for the children. Teachers, principals and county superintendents must not be under any obligations to the mill owners, as such, but be free to carry out the policies in the interests of the children. A law should be passed requiring the title of all school buildings and grounds to be with the county or special school district.

2. The failure of so many thirteen-year-old children to attend school points unmistakably to the lack of efficiency in the enforcement of the compulsory attendance law. When a large per cent of those who by law should attend school are not enrolled it is very probable that the attendance of those who are enrolled is unsatisfactory. The state should require by law a part-time attendance officer for every school system with an enrollment of 200 or more. One county welfare officer alone cannot do this work efficiently.

3. The child, who enters school at six and finishes each grade in a seven-year system, is only thirteen years of age at the com-

pletion of this course. The compulsory attendance law still requires him to attend one more year of school, but the law does not provide him facilities for this extra year. Every school district should be required to provide adequate opportunity for at least eight years of school work. If it is not practical to do this within the school district, then the child should without cost to him for tuition or transportation be given this opportunity elsewhere.

4. To check the tendency in mill schools of children withdrawing from school the day they become fourteen years of age, there should be an educational as well as an age requirement for the child employment similar to that which already exists in thirty other states. By such requirements the attitude of many children toward school work would also be improved.

5. The compulsory attendance upper age limit in North Carolina is the lowest existing among the states and should be raised.

6. The law should require city school districts to include all territory that is within their municipal limits. This would at once give several mill children the school advantages and opportunities of city children. As the tendency of cities in North Carolina to annex outlying territory is very pronounced, the mill schools with limited educational opportunities on the borders of cities would soon be absorbed into city systems with their superior facilities for education.

SOCIAL

Satisfactory solutions of the educational problems of mill villages cannot be approximated until certain unfavorable social conditions are ameliorated. The effect on the education of the child made by the home and community environment may neutralize the beneficial effects of a well-organized school program. An atmosphere characterized by the suppression of discussion and the stifling of initiative is not conducive to the development of democratic ideals. A development and a potency of public opinion are basal to the growth of an efficient system for mill villages. The peculiar social conditions of mill villagers at present inhibit the development of school spirit and community pride.

Some common conditions mostly peculiar to the mill villages need to be modified or changed before the children of these villages cease to be penalized in educational, social and vocational opportunities by living in mill villages.

1. The segregation of mill workers in district areas just without cities or in mill villages, such as those which have been described, tends toward class cleavage. Separate schools of an inferior sort, restrictions upon the exercise of civic functions, separate churches, company stores and the lack of social and business relations with those in other sections are direct results of this segregation, and they emphasize differences. In view of the existing two distinct social classes and the aristocratic social traditions of the South, there is danger of the formation of an intermediate social class of semi-skilled mill workers unless the results of segregation are counteracted. While the division between this class and the upper class may not always be sharply marked, yet it will be definite enough to handicap mill children in the beginning of their careers.

2. If mill workers were encouraged to own their homes, there would likely be an increase in community interests and civic pride among them. The control of mill owners would be lessened. There would soon be permanent residents in the villages to participate in the formation of school policies and to serve as school officials. The interests of mill workers as patrons of the school would likely become articulate.

3. The secret ballot would deprive mill owners of an effectual instrument in influencing the vote of employees in all elections on school questions. The political power of the mill officials would decline in the county and the state if mill employees could vote their convictions without the apprehension of being held to account for their votes. Under the present election law, with little effort the mill owner can ascertain accurately just how employees voted on any measure. It is unwise for those who have such powerful means of control over workmen to be given opportunity to check up on the votes of their employees.

4. Mill villages of 1,000 population or more should be encouraged to become incorporated and thereby self-governing in municipal affairs. The policy of paternalism would be weakened and individual responsibility encouraged. The direct result would be to supply a motive for the discussion and the study of community problems among the residents of the villages. The problems of the means, purposes and opportunities of education would inevitably receive more attention. Playgrounds, libraries and community buildings where there might be uncensored discussion

could be secured. An environment more favorable for civic and social education could be expected from such training in self-government.

An adequate educational program for mill schools must include the community as well as the school. Reports from principals indicate that parents are directly responsible, as much as the mill owners, for the proportionately small attendance at high schools, for the high rate of educational mortality in the early teens; and for the lack of wholesome school spirit and appreciation of school opportunities. Mill workers with little or no education do not appreciate the value of the education of the child. Parents must be educated to a considerable extent before worthy educational standards will obtain in the education of children. The chief obstacle at present, which prevents the coöperation of mill parents in the education of their children is that they consider the children as immediate economic contributors rather than those to whom they should provide further opportunities for growth and development.

An understanding on the part of the parents of the desirability and necessity of their children having better educational facilities than seemed to be necessary when the parents went to school is an objective that must be secured by direct, purposeful agencies. The means to be used are evening schools, parent-teacher associations, lectures, well-chosen films and the use of other sources of publicity. Community or school libraries or both must be provided and reading encouraged.

The type of school organization must be adapted to the mill village situation. The educational and achievement tests given to the children of mill schools revealed the fact that the children of mill villages stood very low in general intelligence; however, they are quite near the standards of their respective grades in fundamentals in arithmetic and not alarmingly below these standards in reading. The investigation of the course of study in the grades revealed that the school program in the vast majority of cases consisted only of the traditional subjects. The program in the light of the results of the intelligence testing must be such as to enrich the experience of the children and to make good the deficiencies of home and community environment now comparatively barren of educative material. The first aim of the school curriculum must be to increase the stock of useful and general information of mill children as far as this can be done by the educational activities and facilities of an efficient school organization.

In view of the home and social environment of the children and the low scores made on general intelligence tests, the method and organization of mill schools should aim to develop initiative and stimulate and encourage broader social and intellectual interests. From the beginning to the end of the course of study, there must be an enrichment by activities and interests beyond the minimum essentials. Suggestions will be made as to how this may be done.

1. In one of the largest mill schools, there are 167 children in school recorded as five years of age. The eleven-year-old pupils in this school tested very low in general intelligence. The small proportion of thirteen-year-old children and those older in school indicated that the five-year-old children were not there because of keen interest in the education of the children. In several other schools, it was evident from the appearance of the children that several were five years old, although they were reported as six. The reasons for sending children to school so early are two: one is that, quite often, the mother as well as the father works in the mill; the other is that there is nothing in the home to keep the child interested, so that it is a relief to have him in school. The needed remedy here is obvious, that of a well-organized kindergarten. The plays, games and other activities of the kindergarten would be the means of enriching the experience of the children and supplying general information which they would otherwise not obtain.

2. One out of every six seven-grade mill schools reporting had no school library. The eleven-grade systems reporting libraries usually had them only for the use of high school pupils. Only seven schools reported libraries with more than 600 volumes. With reading material lacking in the home, with no community library and with inadequate school libraries, a low rating on general intelligence was to be expected. Another means of achieving the needed objective of general intelligence will be the supplying of supplementary reading material, well-chosen and adequate libraries with some juvenile current literature for the elementary grades. A taste for reading and means to gratify it, beginning in

the elementary grades, is an objective to be held constantly in view by those who would improve the educational conditions of mill villages.

3. The type of organization best adapted to mill conditions for the upper grades will be tested in terms of its efficiency both to supply the elements shown by the tests to be most lacking and to hold the largest proportion of upper grades in school. A comparison of the proportion of thirteen- and fourteen-year-old children in the eleven-, nine- and seven-grade systems showed that the lead of the nine-grade system over the other two in holding thirteen-year-old children in school was a decided one. There was also a slight lead in proportion of fourteen-year-old children held. Reasoning based on the facts in the mill situation would tend to confirm the opinion that this lead was not accidental.

The upper compulsory age-limit is an important element in the situation. A child entering school at six and progressing normally will have finished the seventh grade at the end of his twelfth year. If he is in a seven-grade system, he will not likely care to repeat the work. If he is in the system with a four years' course beyond the seventh grade, he sees that he will have to attend three years beyond the compulsory age limit to finish the course. In a nine-year system, there will be only one year beyond the compulsory age limit to finish. He will be more likely to take the chance on one year than three. The type of organization best fitted to hold children beyond the compulsory age-limit would seem to be one which will not appear at the outset to keep them too long from employment. The child of normal or superior ability is the one to whom high school opportunities are most likely to appeal. That type of curriculum which would begin one year before he reached the compulsory age-limit and end one year afterwards would have the strongest appeal. There is recommended, then, for mill schools a junior high school organization beginning with the seventh grade and ending with the ninth. A certificate should be given upon the completion of this work. The eleven-grade systems could adopt this organization and add a two-year course. After they had stayed in school for nine years, it would seem that children would be more likely to remain for eleven grades than they would at the end of the seventh grade. Under such an organization, there are seven-grade systems which would likely add two years. The six-three plan seems best adapted to the mill village conditions of North Carolina.

Again, the results of the intelligence tests would seem to indicate that there are many more than the usual number of children who would find a four-year high school course of the traditional sort too difficult. On the basis of the results of the intelligence test, there would be more reason for urging the majority of mill children to the completion of this short course. At the end of this course, it would be possible to determine more wisely those who should be urged to continue the full high school course.

The six-three plan is recommended as the minimum length of the course for all mill villages. The required elements of the course of study for this period is suggested with the view of meeting the common needs of all the children. While it is important that in all cases a certificate or diploma be given for the completion of this course, yet it must be understood that the addition of two or three more years of high school work is to be insisted upon as an educational opportunity due mill children who are desirous of and prepared for receiving it. The work given chiefly for college entrance purposes may be postponed with profit until after the six-three course has been completed.

The curriculum of this junior high school should be based on the needs of mill children. Initiative, self-reliance, ability to think and helpful information are peculiarly needed by mill children. The subject matter and planned activities of the course of study must be adapted with the view to securing these objectives. There must be a reason for every subject pursued, justified in terms of its vital contribution to those, who for the most part, will have no further educational opportunities.

The required subjects included in such a curriculum should be:

1. Arithmetic and business accounting
2. Hygiene, general science, and biology
3. English, including composition, literature and good current magazines
4. Political, economic and regional geography
5. Vocational and industrial studies, including manual arts for boys and home economics for girls
6. Organization of boy scouts, girl scouts, self-governing clubs and societies

7. Current events discussed at certain periods
8. History: American, Modern European with certain portions of ancient and medieval
9. Community civics and social problems
10. Physical education, games and athletics
11. Music and art appreciation

An organization with such a curriculum is based on the findings of tests and on the age-grade distribution of mill schools.

4. Well-trained teachers and a capable, well-trained and devoted leadership are basal to the execution of this educational program. How to secure these, however, is not peculiarly a mill problem but one whose solution is sought after in all fields of educational effort.